NEW PRAYERS

MICHEL QUOIST

NEW PRAYERS

Translated by Elizabeth Lovatt-Dolan

CROSSROAD · NEW YORK

1991

The Crossroad Publishing Company
370 Lexington Avenue, New York, NY 10017

Originally published in France by
Les Editions Ouvrières, Paris, under the title *Chemins de Prières*
© 1988 Les Editions Ouvrières

English translation © Gill and Macmillan 1989

Printed in the United States of America

Library of Congress Cataloging-in-Publication Data

Quoist, Michel.
    [Chemins de prières. English]
    New prayers / Michel Quoist.
        p.   cm.
    Translation of : Chemins de prières.
    Originally published : Pathways of prayer. Great Britain : Gill and
Macmillan, 1989.
    ISBN 0-8245-0983-8
    1. Meditations.   2. Prayers.   3. Catholic Church—Prayer-books and
devotions—English.   I. Title.
BX2182.2.Q65313   1990
242'.802—dc20   89-78378
                                                                    CIP

Scripture quotations are from the
Good News Bible, the Bible in Today's English Version.
Copyright © American Bible Society 1966, 1971, 1976.

Contents

Introduction

My dear friends,

We often say to ourselves:
I ought to pray, I have a need to pray,
I want to pray but I simply don't know how,
I would like to pray, but I don't have time.
I wish I could pray more, but I find prayer boring,
I don't have the courage.

The hours go by, the days and weeks pass too quickly or too slowly. And all the time we are aware of this longing, this need to pray, this uneasy feeling deep within us, which can surface when there is a lull in the storms of life, or when failures and hard knocks leave us battered and bruised, and we shout HELP! During these times we search for God, we want to meet him, we want to ask for his help. We try to pray, some of the time we succeed in praying, but it's not easy for us and we are uncertain of the results.

Do you know why we so often feel that with our poor human efforts we are stumbling and failing, our prayers are too short and don't reach a God who seems very distant, a God who seems invisible to us?

Do you know why we are disheartened when our requests are unanswered, when God is silent and there is darkness in our hearts?

Do you know why, in our efforts to learn to pray, we never seem to advance beyond the learning stage?

Do you know why those things that we do repeatedly, that are part of the way we pray—such as familiar words and hymns, whether we stand, kneel or sit, the ritual and the warm feeling when people are gathered together in prayer, the lights and the incense, and the thousand and one formulae we have tried—can turn out eventually to be no more than sad illusions? It is because they are meaningless unless we believe that from the very beginning God has searched us out before we have searched for him, that it is he who prays to us before we pray to him, that it is he who hears our prayers before we put them into words.

St John tells us: 'This is what love is: it is not that we have loved God, but that he loved us and sent his Son . . .' (1 Jn. 4:10)

Those words say it all. God 'so loved the world that he sent his Son . . .' to us. He came a long time ago. He is with us 'always, to the end of the age' (Mt. 28:20). He walks with us. He pleads with us to work with him and with his Spirit of love. But our eyes are closed and all too often we look for him in 'heaven', among the clouds of our imaginings or we get carried away by our sentiments and emotions. When this happens, we are in danger of missing him as he passes by.

Do we believe that God has come among us, in Jesus Christ, a human being like us — Yes or No? If we answer yes, then we must meet him and welcome him and one of the best places to meet him is in the Gospels; not the Gospels understood as a recording of the actual words of Jesus of Nazareth but rather as the core of his message, gathered together by the Apostles, meditated on by the early christian communities and authenticated by the Church. God enters into dialogue with men and women. Their response is one of the main foundations of christian prayer.

But Jesus of Nazareth died. We believe that he rose from the dead. He is alive today. For us, his story is not just ancient history. It is a reality, mysterious to be sure, but a reality that unfolds over time. Jesus is born, lives, suffers, dies and rises again each day in his members. The smallest details of our daily lives, the lives of our brothers and sisters, the whole history of humanity, these also are places of encounter and dialogue between God and humankind.

All too often however, we are blind and we don't see Jesus in the ordinary things of life. We are deaf and we don't hear him challenging us as we go about our daily affairs. We must ask him to heal our blindness and our deafness. Then we will be able to talk to him, ceaselessly linking the whole universe and the whole human family with his action in the world, and little by little our lives will become a loving response to his loving invitation.

Of course there are other ways of praying — liturgy, the sacraments . . . , but if our prayer is not connected to the Gospel and to life we risk ending up in blind alleys which will lead us to illusion and to disillusion. I hope these pages may help some of us to avoid this danger.

For quite a while now, many of the readers of Prayers of Life have been asking for more. I have continued to refuse, because I

2

have no wish at all to substitute my words and my prayers for your words and your prayers. And then there are so many books already! Is there any need for another one?

I gave in eventually, because I know that I am not so much giving you something as returning what the Lord and you yourselves have given to me.

I have been fascinated by Jesus Christ and I try to follow him. He 'speaks' to me through the Gospels and I am nourished by his word. But he also speaks to me through the life that I see around me, the life that you tell me about. I 'keep all these things in my heart' and my words and prayers are simply an attempt to respond.

Some of the words on the pages of this book are mine, some of them are yours, and occasionally they are what I imagine Jesus would be saying to us if we could hear him with our human ears. We have to take the risk of attributing words to Jesus because he has no other way of speaking to us through the complex pattern of our lives. If we are nourished by the Gospel, then gradually our attitudes will become 'Gospel attitudes'. Then we can honestly ask ourselves: 'What is Jesus saying to me today, through this or that bit of my life or the lives of my sisters and brothers?' 'What does he expect of me, of us?' And then it is up to us to respond to him through prayer and through action.

I would like to offer you fine and beautiful words, worthy of the Lord and worthy of you. To fashion and re-fashion them before giving them to you would have called for more time and talent than I have at my disposal. But I console myself, saying that these prayers are only a few 'pathways' to help you, if possible, to continue your pilgrimage towards God who has come into the very centre of our lives in the person of Jesus Christ.

He is waiting for us!

Good journey, my friends! And let's not be so busy looking for him that we fail to notice him as he passes by. May we always be linked to him, through our own lives, through the lives of our brothers and sisters and the life of the world. Then indeed will all of human history become prayer in Jesus Christ.

Michel Quoist

1. Glory to you, my God!

People are always happy to be admired for themselves. Often they are even happier when somebody sincerely acknowledges the importance of their work. Parents are overjoyed when they are complimented on their children.

Why wouldn't God appreciate compliments too? Certainly, we should glorify him for what he is. But we should remember to praise him also for what he does, and especially for his beloved children, the men and women with whom he is always present, rejoicing as they grow in the life he has given them. Some of us tend to forget this and are convinced that the way to please God is to think only of 'Him'.

Glorifying God through men and women who are in the process of becoming is to look at them with the same love and pride as our Father, who watches so closely over his children that 'even the hairs of their heads have all been counted' (Lk. 12:7).

As St Irenaeus says: 'The glory of God is the person fully alive. The life of the person is the vision of God'.

Glory to you, my God!
For the little one learning to walk,
   who lets go of mother's hand,
   falls,
   gets up
   and starts on the adventure all over again;
for the youngster on the bike,
   trying to ride without holding the handlebars,
   and trying twenty more times without succeeding;
for the adolescent worrying over a maths problem
   but sticking with it,
   determined to find the solution alone.

Glory to you, my God!
For the athletes who train every day
   to run faster,
   to jump farther
   and always higher,
   to break their own records;

for the artists who struggle with stone or wood,
    colours or sounds,
    to create new works;
for the researchers who study in the shadows,
    carrying out experiments,
    striving to unlock the secrets of this world
    in which we live together.

    Glory to you, my God!
For the miners who extract iron ore from the ground,
    For the foundry workers,
    and those who make tools
    and machines;
for the architects and for the armies of brick-layers
    who build houses, cathedrals and towns;
for the scholars, engineers and technicians,
    for the multitudes working
    with intellect and hands,
    slowly exploring the world
    and bringing order into life,
for all those committed to the struggle
    for the development of people and peoples,
    and to the building of a just and peaceful world.

    Glory to you, my God!
For man and woman slowly coming to be,
    out of the immensity of time;
since they emerged from the clay,
    you called them to stand upright;
since flesh was illumined by the spark of the spirit,
    you called them to think, to love,
    and to participate in their own creation;
since you gave the universe
    into their liberated hands
    to take possession of it,
    to develop and transform it.

    Glory to you, my God!
For this stupendous and marvellous ascent
of humankind;

for your joy in our growth;
for your humility,
   you who stand back
   instead of taking our place;
for your patience with our slowness,
   our mistakes and our failures.

   And, finally, I give glory to you my God,
because you created men and women free
   and worthy to meet you,
   capable of knowing you
   and of loving you;
because you didn't think it was demeaning
   when you yourself
   became a man
   in your son Jesus;
because through him,
   we can
   call you our Father,
   if we want to,
   and one day we can come to you,
   to live in your love
   and your joy forever.

You are the light of the world!

A city built on a hill cannot be hidden. No one lights a lamp and puts it under a bowl; instead he puts it on the lampstand, where it gives light for everyone in the house. In the same way your light must shine before people, so that they will see the good things you do and praise your Father in heaven (Mt 5:14–16).

To him who by means of his power working in us is able to do so much more than we can ever ask for, or even think of: to God be the glory in the church and in Christ Jesus for all time, for ever and ever! Amen (Eph. 3:20–21).

2. Lord,
Why do we always have to make an effort?
. . . I don't feel like it

Many young people, and some not so young, base their activities entirely on what they feel like doing or would prefer not to do in particular circumstances. Some just don't want to make an effort. Others are convinced that if they don't feel like doing something it is often better not to do it at all. They think that they are being untrue to themselves if they do something simply because they are forced to do it. They think that is just pretending, especially in relation to God: 'I don't see why I should smile at somebody, pray, or go to Mass, if I don't feel like it . . .!'
This attitude arises from a misunderstanding of the meaning of freedom. Respecting children's freedom does not always mean allowing them to do whatever they want to do.
The freedom that the Lord offers us is not the freedom to do anything that comes into our heads. What he offers us is the freedom to love authentically, ourselves, others and God, regardless of how we feel.
Jesus didn't 'feel like' dying for us.

Lord,
why do we always have to make an effort?
. . . . I don't feel like it.

I don't feel like getting up
    and I don't feel like going to bed,
I don't feel like going to work
    or like going to college.
I don't feel like doing the housework
    and I don't feel like doing the ironing.
I don't feel like turning off the TV
    and doing my home-work.
I don't feel like keeping quiet
    or like talking.

7

I don't feel like going to see this person
    or shaking hands with him
    or even smiling at him.
I don't feel like putting my arms around him.
I don't feel like giving the help I've been asked for,
    I don't want to commit myself,
    and I don't feel like going to that meeting.
I don't feel like resisting the side-roads
    which tempt me to stray from my path,
    or like switching off the golden images
    that are projected non-stop
    on the screen of my dreams.
I don't feel like struggling against time,
    pausing,
    reflecting,
    meditating on your word,
    and I don't feel like praying.

Lord,
why do we always have to make an effort,
    to live each day
    as you want us to live it?
It's not easy,
it's not much fun.
So often, what I feel like doing
    is just what I oughtn't to do,
    and what I ought to do
    is what I don't feel like doing!
Lord,
Is it true that we must always make an effort?
. . . even when we don't feel a bit like it!

My child, says the Lord,
    it is true
that the seed must be watered every day
    if it is to grow into a tree,
that the mother must labour at the birthing
    and the parents with the upbringing
    if the child is to become an adult,
    that the baker must work during the night

8

if the dough is to rise,
and the workers must stay on the assembly line
    if the car is to run,
    . . . even if they don't feel like it.

It is true,
that scientists must search for a long time
    to find the medicine that heals,
that men and women must sacrifice their lives
    so that justice may come,
and that lovers must die every day to their own selfish
                                        desires
    so that love may live
    . . . even if they don't feel like it.

For where would your dignity be, my little one,
    your wonderful freedom
    and your power to love,
if the Father were to give you trees and children fully
                                        formed,
    and bread served up on the table ready to eat,
    and life-saving medicines that could never fail,
    and the world like a paradise for a peaceful humanity,
    and love in full flower
    that would never fade?

It is hard to be a human being,
    and it is hard to be a loving person,
I know.
I didn't want to spend thirty years
    climbing the steps of Calvary,
but it was my Father's wish that my whole life
    should be offered to you.
And I loved you, my brothers and sisters,
    and I made the effort
    to go up on the cross,
    so that all of your efforts
    might, one day, be crowned with *life*.

Go, little one,
don't ask yourself how you feel about doing this or that,
ask if it is what the Father wants
    for you and for your brothers and sisters.
Don't ask me for the strength to make the effort;
ask first to love with all your strength,
    your God and your brothers and sisters,
because if you loved a little more
    you would suffer much less,
and if you loved much more
    your suffering would bring forth *joy*
    and *life*.

Now, what do you think? There was once a man who had two sons. He went to the elder one and said, 'Son, go and work in the vineyard today.' 'I don't want to,' he answered, but later he changed his mind and went. Then the father went to the other son and said the same thing. 'Yes sir' he answered, but he did not go. Which one of the two did what his father wanted?
'The elder one' they answered.
So Jesus said to them, 'I tell you: the tax collectors and the prostitutes are going into the Kingdom of God ahead of you' (Mt. 21:28–31).

Then Jesus called the crowd and his disciples to him. 'If anyone wants to come with me,' he told them, 'he must forget self, carry his cross, and follow me. For whoever wants to save his own life will lose it; but whoever loses his life for me and for the gospel will save it. Does a person gain anything if he wins the whole world but loses his life? Of course not! There is nothing he can give to regain his life' (Mk. 8: 34–37).

3. Open my eyes, Lord!

The world and humanity challenge us and disturb us. We would like to know everything there is to be known about them, about what lies beyond our own horizons. But we only see the surface of things and of human beings. To go deeper and to see as God sees, we need a different way of looking. Only 'the eyes of faith'—in other words, the eyes of Jesus Christ grafted onto our human eyes—can bring us his light and enable us to undertake this long pilgrimage.

Then, little by little, we will see the Spirit of Jesus working throughout the course of human history and in its smallest details, and we will see his great Body which is born, develops, dies and rises each day. No longer will we contemplate simply Jesus of Nazareth, but Christ unfolding in the course of history his mystery of Creation, Incarnation and Redemption, and we can be joined to him through every part of our lives and that of our brothers and sisters, to work with him and to build up his Father's kingdom.

Lord,
I wish you would give me immense eyes
    to look at the world!
Because I'm looking, Lord.
I like looking,
    but my eyes are small,
    too small
to see what lies beyond things,
    men and women and events.

I look and I wonder about life,
    but I see only the outer shell
    which is hard and sometimes rough.
Love beckons,
    but I contemplate
    only some of the flowers and fruits,
    while the vital spirit escapes me.
And I suffer behind the thick glass of my window,
    I bang into it

11

and sometimes I hurt myself badly,
when a mist rises in my heart
   and clouds my way.
Lord, why have you given us eyes
   that can't see,
   can't see your *life* beyond life,
your *love* beyond love?

Sometimes, I seem to catch a few glimmers
   and then, mysteriously,
   words somewhat more beautiful
   than ordinary words
   are born in my heart,
words which dance and whirl,
trying to escape from their gilded cage.
   They fly from my lips
   and I attempt to catch them,
   to tell myself and to express
   what I'm wondering about. . .
   what I expect. . .
   what I'm getting near. . .
   without being able to grasp it.
But the words are little birds, too small;
I hold it against them that they don't know how to sing
   the song of the infinite,
   for me and for others.

Then, sometimes,
I close my eyes willingly, for a long while,
and in the quiet of the night
   I catch a glimpse of
a little of that light
that is hidden from me by day.
   Then I *see* without seeing,
   I *believe.*

But, Lord, you have given me
eyes to look at my brothers and sisters,
   feet to walk towards them,
   and to tread the good earth with them!

Lord, can I walk with my eyes closed,
shutting out the day?
　　I want to *see* when I look,
but my eyes are small,
　　too small
　　to contemplate what lies beyond.
Lord, give me immense eyes
　　to look at the world.

　　Open my eyes, Lord,
　　that I may *see*. . .
farther than the light of the rising sun,
which suddenly tinges nature
with the soft gleam of a young girl's face;
farther than the light of the setting sun,
　　when streaks of night sketch
　　the shadow of wrinkles on the earth,
like the years on a weather-beaten face. . .
　　that at last I may *see*
　　the reflection of your infinite *light*.

　　Open my eyes, Lord,
　　that I may *see*. . .
beyond the radiance of the silently smiling rose,
beyond the hand that offers it to me,
and the heart beyond the hand,
and the care that goes beyond even the heart,
　　. . . that I may see, at last,
　　the reflection of your *love*.

　　Open my eyes, Lord,
　　that I may see. . .
beyond human bodies
　　which attract or repel,
beyond their eyes and their glances
which light up or become dim,
　　troubled hearts,
　　joyous hearts.
And farther than the hearts of flesh,
　　the flowers of love,

and even the wild grasses
   that we so quickly name as sins,
   . . . that I may *see*, at last,
   the children of the good God,
   coming into the world and growing up
   beneath the loving gaze of Our Father.

   Open my eyes, Lord,
   that I may *see*. . .
farther than the roads used by heavy trucks,
   the night,
when a thousand lights escape from hot factories;
farther than the ribbons of smoke
   tossed by the wind,
   above chimneys
   pointed towards the unattainable sky,
beyond those disturbing beauties,
   cities of the year 2000,
where man and woman ceaselessly remake the face of the
                                                    earth,
   . . . that I may *see*, at last, and *hear*
   the heartbeat of thousands of workers
   who complete creation with you.

   Open my eyes, Lord,
   that I may *see*. . .
beyond the inextricable dove-tailing
of human roads without number,
   roads that go uphill or down,
   express-ways or blind alleys,
   red traffic lights,
   green traffic lights,
   'no entry' signs and 'speed limit' signs;
roads east, west, north or south,
   roads leading to Rome,
   to Jerusalem,
   or to Mecca,
farther than the millions who have travelled them
for thousands of years,
and farther than the stupendous mystery of their freedom,

14

which casts them,
thinking,
loving,
on the paths of life
leading to the cross-roads of their destiny,
. . . that I may *see*
your Calvary raised on high,
overlooking the central cross-roads of the world,
and YOU,
down from your cross,
risen from the dead and travelling all these roads of
Emmaus,
where so many men and women walk alongside you
without recognising you,
except for the few, in your Word
and in the breaking of bread;
that I may finally *see*
your great Body growing,
in the breath of the Spirit
and with Mary's motherly help,
until that day when you present yourself to the Father,
at the end of time,
when you, my great Jesus,
will have reached
your full height.

But I know, Lord, that in this world
I must see without seeing,
and that as long as I am on this earth
I will be a pilgrim of the invisible with heart unsatisfied.
I know also that it is not until tomorrow,
when I pass through the portals of night
and see you at last as you really are,
in your light,
that I will *see* what you see.[1]

1. 1 Jn. 3:2

I must wait a while longer and walk in the half-light. . .
But if it is your will, Lord,
   that this my prayer,
   confided to so many friends
   who will share it,
should not be just so many empty words,
   I beg you,
   I beseech you,
give us immense eyes
to look at the world,
   and we will see a little of what lies beyond,
   and those who look at us
   will see what you see.
Then, perhaps, we will be able to say to them at last:
   It is he, Jesus Christ
   the Light of the World.

They came to Bethsaida, where some people brought a blind man to Jesus and begged him to touch him. Jesus took the blind man by the hand and led him out of the village. After spitting on the man's eyes, Jesus placed his hands on him and asked, 'Can you see anything?'
The man looked up and said, 'Yes, I can see people, but they look like trees walking about.'
Jesus again placed his hands on the man's eyes. This time the man looked intently, his eyesight returned and he saw everything clearly' (Mk. 8:22–25).

By speaking the truth in a spirit of love, we must grow up in every way to Christ, who is the head. Under his control all the different parts of the body fit together, and the whole body is held together by every joint with which it is provided. So when each separate part works as it should, the whole body grows and builds itself up through love (Eph. 4:15–16).

Christ is like a single body, which has many parts; it is still one body, even though it is made up of different parts. In the same way, all of us, whether Jews or Gentiles, whether slaves or free, have been baptized into the one body by the same Spirit, and we have all been given the one Spirit to drink (1 Cor. 12:12–13).

16

4. The Monday wash

As he walked the roads of Palestine, Jesus observed the life going on around him. Especially the life of ordinary people: the woman making bread, the woman searching for a lost coin; the injured man who had been attacked on the road, the children playing and the widow weeping; the sower in the field, the good harvest, and the shepherd with his flock . . . as he observed, he was filled with wonder. He saw the seeds of the Kingdom sprouting already through all this life.
Jesus is still travelling our human roads today: 'I will be with you always, to the end of the age' (Mt. 28:20). He beckons to us, unobtrusively. Wherever there is the smallest gesture of genuine love, he is there: '. . . love comes from God. Whoever loves is a child of God and knows God'. (1 Jn. 4:7) It is up to us to follow in his footsteps through the thousands of little things that constitute a fruitful existence if they are nourished by this love.

Lord,
today is Monday.
I went out and I saw laundry drying,
   hanging at the windows
   and on balconies,
here and there in the concrete hollow,
   a motley mosaic,
   sparkling with colour against the grey of the buildings.

The wind was making the multi-coloured notes sing
   on the clothes-line,
and whispering in the ear of my heart, I heard
   the song of trouble
   and the song of love.

Dirty clothes,
clean clothes,
dried clothes,
ironed clothes, soiled again,
to be washed again,

dried again,
ironed again.

Clothes for my husband,
clothes for my son,
clothes for my daughter,
and my own mixed in with them.

Clothes for one week to the next,
from one washing to the next,
from one drying to the next,
from one ironing to the next.

Lord,
I offer you this evening,
for all those women who don't know you,
or for all who don't think of praying to you,
this washing which is whiter,
smoother,
softer,
this washing scented with the love of mothers
and of wives.

I offer you all these daily acts,
repeated a thousand times over,
making up the fabric of beautiful hidden lives,
the wonderful lives of humble people
who know that to love is to endure,
beyond weariness.

Little one, have I told you?
I'm telling you now
and you are to tell your brothers and sisters:
'The Kingdom of God is like a woman,
who spends her whole life
turning dirty washing into clean washing,
not through the power of some miracle detergent,
but through the miracle of love,
given every day.'

Jesus told them another parable:
'The Kingdom of heaven is like this. A man takes a mustard seed and sows it in his field. It is the smallest of all seeds, but when it grows up, it is the biggest of all plants. It becomes a tree, so that birds come and make their nests in its branches.'
Jesus told them still another parable:
'The Kingdom of heaven is like this. A woman takes some yeast and mixes it with forty litres of flour until the whole batch of dough rises' (Mt. 13:31–33).

A teacher of the law came up and tried to trap Jesus. 'Teacher,' he asked, 'what must I do to receive eternal life?' Jesus answered him, 'What do the Scriptures say? How do you interpret them?' The man answered, 'Love the Lord your God with all your heart, with all your soul, with all your strength, and with all your mind'; and 'Love your neighbour as you love yourself.' (Lk. 10:25–27)

5. It would be so easy, Lord . . .

Many activists in the Church today are tired. They find them-selves up against so many difficulties and misunderstandings that they would like to draw back, to take a rest.

Then again, there are young people who announce that they have no intention of doing as their parents did. They want to have time to live, time for themselves.

Finally, some of the most committed people think that they may even be on the wrong road, that they ought to pray more and . . . leave the action to God.

This state of affairs is serious, very serious. God did not give us men and women, humanity, a world, 'off the shelf'; he gave them to be created by us. There is no way that christians can retire to their tents and refuse to take on this task. More than any others, they are called to take it on, according to their possibilities. This is the indisputable criterion of the authenticity of their love for their brothers and sisters.

To have a living faith does not mean that we run away from the building site to ask God to do our work for us. It means that we give all our energies to the job on hand, while asking God to work with us.

It would be so easy, Lord,
to abandon the struggle for a better world . . .
    this world which is still being born!
    It would be so easy
to give up the exhausting meetings,
    the discussions,
    the reports,
the innumerable actions and commitments
    that are supposed to be essential,
and the evenings of utter weariness,
    when I am more and more doubtful
    about how they can possibly help my brothers and sisters.

    It would be so easy
to listen to those voices around me,
voices that seem wise, friendly

20

and even affectionate,
voices saying to me:
  'You're getting excited',
  You're banging your head against a wall',
  'You're missing the point';
  voices whispering insidiously behind my back:
  'He enjoys that',
  'That's his temperament',
  'He doesn't like to be passed over'.

It would be so easy
to give way to discouragement,
and to dress it up in the good and pious intentions
  of forgotten obligations
  and broken promises.

It would be so easy then
to withdraw to my own home,
to have free evenings again,
and week-ends to enjoy,
  and children's laughter,
  and my wife's arms.

It would be so easy to sit down
and bandage my wounds after too many hard fights,
  to rest my tired legs,
  my arms, my head,
  and my heart,
and to find peace far from the din of battle,
and to listen at last to the silence
  in which you speak to the faithful—so they say—
  far away from the noise.

It would be easier, Lord,
to stand aside and not to get my hands dirty,
to watch others fighting and debating,
to advise them and to complain about them,
to judge them . . . and to pray for them.
  It would be easier . . .
  but I ask you, Lord,

is that really what you want of me?
    I no longer know.
    I no longer know.

    Lord, enlighten me, help me.
    I no longer know what I should do,
because in the concert of voices around me,
    wise voices,
    friends' voices,
    and those of my dear ones,
I often hear another voice,
    deeper and more serious,
    challenging me, persistently,
    in the depths of my troubled heart:
'You are taking the Lord's place.
Only he can change men and women and the world.
    Abandon yourself to him
    and he will do what you,
    in your arrogance,
    thought you were capable of doing.'

Is this your voice, Lord?
    I don't know any longer.
    I don't know any longer.
    . . . But if this is really what you want, this evening,
    I place my resignation in your hands!

I refuse to accept your resignation, says the Lord,
    Don't listen to your voices,
    they don't come from me.
    I will never take your place,
    because it is I who have given it to you.
Nothing will be done without you and without your
                            brothers and sisters,
because I have wanted you to be responsible together
    for humankind and for the world.
But nothing will be done without me either . . .
and perhaps you have forgotten that.

Go now, little one, and sleep in peace,
   and tomorrow,
   you and I,
   I and you,
   together,
   both of us with your sisters and brothers,
   we will take up the struggle again.

Then Jesus' mother and brothers arrived. They stood outside the house and sent in a message, asking for him. A crowd was sitting round Jesus, and they said to him, 'Look, your mother and your brothers and sisters are outside, and they want you.' Jesus answered. 'Who is my mother? Who are my brothers?' He looked at the people sitting round him and said, 'Look! Here are my mother and my brothers! Whoever does what God wants him to do is my brother, my sister, my mother' (Mk. 3:31–35).

Not everyone who calls me 'Lord, Lord' will enter the Kingdom of heaven, but only those who do what my Father in heaven wants them to do' (Mt. 7:21).

6. Lord,
Are you coming shopping with me?

Jesus Christ waits for us, faithfully, at the very centre of our lives. Far too often, we have the idea that if we want to pray to him we have to stop all activity so as to give ourselves completely to him. Of course there are times when this is what we ought to do. We should remember, however, that there is no better way of expressing love than by just being with a person, without doing anything for or with that person, but simply offering the gift of ten or fifteen minutes out of our lives, freely. But we should also accompany Jesus on the roadways of the world. Our lives in their entirety could become 'prayer' if we realized that he came among us, not to stay all the time in the background but to be the yeast in the dough of every aspect of our lives and the lives of our sisters and brothers.

I had to go out shopping,
    but once again
    I was regretting the time it took,
    time wasted, I thought.
Oh, the tyranny of time,
    imposed partner,
implacable companion of my days and years,
    it breaks up my life,
    hurries me and rules me,
    runs so fast
    and makes me run!
Am I not the slave of time?

But this morning, Lord, you beckoned to me,
reminding me that you were there.
    Available,
    peaceful,
    just standing still.
I decided then to get time under control,
    to take my time,
to leave my car behind and to go on foot.
And I said to you, Lord:

'Are you coming shopping with me?'
We shopped together,
and this evening I want to thank you for coming with me,
    because I saw things I would never have noticed
    if you hadn't been there.
I saw streams of life
    in my neighbourhood streets,
    cars moving along
    and drivers getting impatient,
    people in a hurry
    and people strolling.
I saw the angry mother
dragging her crying child,
    and the one
    who stopped for a few moments
    to smile and talk to her baby;
the unemployed person seeking help,
and the lady walking her little pet dog;
the young people embracing each other,
and the children shouting and squabbling
as they came out from school.
I saw the shop-windows,
    welcoming,
    enticing,
and the longing looks piercing the glass
to caress a thousand scraps of earthly paradise,
the posters proclaiming the joys of life,
    and others announcing the struggle
    of people battling for survival.

And I said to you:
Look, Lord,
    you see this person here
    and that one there,
tell them that you love them;
    yes, say it,
to those who are unaware that you accompany them,
    step by step,
    every day.

And as for me, Lord, you allowed me to watch them with
you,
and I saw them, for a little while,
    as you see them.

I saw their joys and their sorrows,
    beyond the look in their eyes
    and the patter of their footsteps;
I saw your life in their life,
    your love in their loves,
    despite their ignorance
    and perhaps even their rejection of you.
Through you, I saw them as brothers and sisters,
called to say together, one day:
'Our Father who art in heaven'.
There were times
    when I thought you weren't there . . .
but that's not my fault, Lord,
because so often you are silent!
You know I complain about your silence
    and that I suffer because of it,
    oh, so much!

But now,
I know that the strongest love
    is not the most vociferous,
and I believe in your love.
I came home happy,
    I had overcome time,
    I hadn't wasted my time,
    and I'm sure
that you were happy too,
because there are people with great minds, Lord, who say
    that if we want to pray to you we must:
    go away by ourselves,
    kneel down or sit up straight,
    with our arms here
    and our hands there,
close our eyes to see you better
and our ears to hear you better,

and begin by . . .
and continue by . . .
and finish by . . .
but they forget to say, Lord,
that we should go out occasionally,
to go shopping with you
   and to look at the world,
   at men and women,
   at life,
so as to gather up the joys of all these people,
   and their secret sorrows,
and give them to you to carry,
because you gladly bear the heaviest burdens
   and leave the lighter packages to us.

Lord,
you restored sight to the blind
   and hearing to the deaf.
Yet again, I implore you,
   open my eyes,
   open my ears.
So often, I'm tempted to turn in on myself
and to shop without seeing and hearing.
With you,
   I'll shop with my heart.
And when I get back home, I'll be rich,
   not with what I've bought,
   but with what I've seen,
   received,
   carried.
In the evening, I'll open my bag in front of our Father,
   to show my shopping to him
and—excuse me Lord—
   if I produce some damaged fruit
   that I took a fancy to while I was out,
   thinking it was edible,
I'll give it to you
and you will burn it with your love.

Jesus went round visiting all the towns and villages. He taught in the synagogues, preached the Good News about the Kingdom, and healed people with every kind of disease and sickness. As he saw the crowds, his heart was filled with pity for them, because they were worried and helpless, like sheep without a shepherd. So, he said to his disciples, 'The harvest is large, but there are few workers to gather it in. Pray to the owner of the harvest that he will send out workers to gather in his harvest' (Mt. 9:35–38).

Jesus spoke . . . again. 'I am the light of the world,' he said. 'Whoever follows me will have the light of life and will never walk in darkness' (Jn. 8:12).

7. It's too heavy, Lord, I can't carry this weight any longer

The baggage that each one of us carries with us in our minds is often filled with painful memories, sufferings, sins, which we have collected on our journey through life and continue to drag along with us. Small sufferings, severe trials, and sometimes deep secrets that we thought were locked away forever.

We try to forget, because we think this is the right thing to do: 'One oughtn't to cling to the past'; or to have peace: 'I don't want to think about it any more'. We keep all of it buried. But every-thing we have experienced remains alive inside us, even if we have succeeded in pushing our memories right back into into the unconscious.

When this life is locked away inside us it goes bad, it affects our behaviour . . . it makes us ill.

Christians, we are like the child who, though scarcely able to lift a load, still tries to carry it without help from anybody. Father is there, walking alongside. But the child refuses his offer of help, struggles on alone, falls sometimes and is badly hurt.

Our father is God. In his son Jesus Christ he came to carry our sufferings, our sins . . . but we have to give them to him. And the way to give them is not by forgetting them, but by having the courage to dig them out, to look straight at them, and to accept them. This is the price we must pay if we want to be free to live our lives through the risen Christ.

It's too heavy, Lord,
 I can't carry this weight any longer!
But, this evening, I think I have discovered at last
 what you have wanted of me
 for a long time.

My life's journey doesn't stretch very far, Lord,
 but my past is laden down.
I have had so many hard knocks in the course of my travels,
 and experienced so many things
 that have hurt me,
 that have upset me,

or have engraved this pitiless remorse on my soul,
and suffering heaped on suffering
　　has accumulated in my heart.
　　The attics are stuffed with them
　　and the cellars are full.
And right at the bottom, like a corpse in the earth,
　　is this deep secret . . .
—a secret that belongs to me or to a dear one—
　　trampled under foot a thousand times,
　　covered again a thousand times,
　　but always stirring
　　just when I think I have buried it forever.

It's too heavy, Lord,
　　I can't carry this weight any longer!

The load is too heavy
　　and my back aches.
I'm worried sick
　　and my liver is giving me trouble.
I can't digest these sufferings
　　and I have a pain in my stomach.

And all these things, Lord,
　　which take away my appetite,
　　which make me fret,
　　which paralyse me,
　　which give me a stomach-ache,
　　which make me deaf or blind . . .
all these heart-aches
which make my body hurt,
　　and leave me feeling weak,
　　depressed,
　　prevent me from sleeping . . .
　　and from waking up . . .
I just had to get rid of them, Lord,
　　because the load is too heavy,
　　I can't carry it any longer.

I've tried everything . . .
    in vain.

I've been told, Lord,
that small troubles go away very quickly
    and great sorrows are dimmed with the passage of time;
that I should be brave and not think about it any more,
because the past is past and should be forgotten.
    You know that I tried.
I have tried time and time again to turn over the page
    so that I could no longer see it,
but whenever there was a breath of wind
the photo album of my old memories opened up again.

I have tried to heal my wounds
    with a thousand sorts of balm,
    with beautiful ideas
    and lovely sentiments,
and even with great bursts of faith and constant prayer.
    But whenever there was the slightest upset in my life,
    old sores opened.
    They bled.
    I had to begin all over again!

For a while I thought I had finally succeeded.
With some pride I said. 'That's it, it's over and done with',
    because I've accepted everything and stopped thinking
                                        about it . . .
but the buried memories and sufferings
    were still alive inside me.
    Like wild plants,
    their roots are still there,
    and when I try to pull them up,
    with leaves and fruit,
they spring up again painfully
in the recesses of my heart.
    They are watered by my tears.
    They come to the surface.
    They invade me,

suffocate me,
eat into my life,
leave me depressed,
and seep through
the core of my being,
these thick walls
which I thought were safe from infiltration,
but the repressed and painful memories
break through violently and overwhelm me.

And sometimes, Lord,
I believe I'm free.
The painful memories are gone . . . !
At long last I'm able to sleep.
But during the night, alas,
my body keeps thrashing around,
because the ghosts of these memories
emerge from their hiding-places
and dance their fandangoes
in my dreams or my nightmares.
I wake up tired.
I get up exhausted.

It's too heavy, Lord.
I can't carry this weight any longer.

But this evening . . .
am I dreaming, Lord?
I think I have finally discovered
what you have wanted of me for a long time.
Just by chance,
I happened to read this sentence from a psalm
printed on a holy picture:
'Cast your burden on the Lord
and he will sustain you' (Ps. 55:22).
And I believe you have spoken to me
through these words.

Forgive me, Lord,
for all this lost time,

for all the suffering
   and discouragement,
for the awful grief
   and the frantic protests,
   consequences of the life which was locked in,
   pressed down,
   spoiled
   and rotting in my heart,
   the special compost heap of my own weeds.

Forgive me, Lord, because you were there,
you were waiting to carry the burden with me
   . . . and to carry the heaviest bit
like a father helping his own little one,
and leaving in the child's hands
   exactly what such a little one is able to lift.

But I didn't see you
   because I was wrapped up in my own suffering.
I didn't hear you
   because I was listening to the sound of my tears,
   and alone,
   in my arrogance,
   I wanted to keep it all to myself.

Forgive me, Lord, because you were there.
You were waiting to take me in your arms,
   to lift me up,
   to carry me,
and to carry my baggage at the same time.

But finally, Lord,
I had to accept all that I had experienced
and I had to give it to you freely,
because you don't take by force
what a person doesn't want to give you.

Here I am at last,
before you, Lord,
   out of breath,
   at death's door.

I want to give you *everything*
   . . . but without your help, Lord,
   I know
that I won't be able to give you all of me.

Help me, Lord, I beg you,
because it's going to take me a long time
to uproot everything
   without snatching any of it back again;
a lot of effort to move everything
   without holding onto anything
   that I would like to keep for myself;
a lot of humility to reveal
   all that I wanted to hide.
It will take me a long time
to become accustomed to giving you
all the pebbles as well as the stones from my path,
   the ones I stumble over, every day,
   the ones that are thrown at me by others,
   thoughtlessly or spitefully,
   the ones that I throw at others,
   and that are returned to me.

Help me, Lord,
in the difficulties of life,
   yesterday's
   and today's,
to look fearlessly
   instead of averting my eyes,
to unearth
   rather than to bury,
to have the courage to remember
   instead of trying to forget,
and to feel what I have experienced
   instead of repressing it.
Because it is only when I am ready to give
that I can confide to you
   the things I am holding in my trembling hands,
   and you are always there,
   waiting to free me from them.

It's too heavy, Lord,
 I can't carry this weight any longer. . .
 but you have invited me
to empty the baggage of hurtful and painful memories,
every evening.
 Then I will be
like a little child in his father's arms,
 in his mother's arms,
who has told them all his troubles
and then drops off to sleep peacefully,
 because he knows he is loved,
 and the love of his parents
 is the strongest thing he knows.

Cast your burden on the Lord and he will sustain you (Ps. 55:22).

I place myself in your care. You will save me, Lord; you are a faithful God (Ps. 31:5).

Come to me, all of you who are tired from carrying heavy loads, and I will give you rest. Take my yoke and put it on you, and learn from me, because I am gentle and humble in spirit; and you will find rest. For the yoke I will give you is easy, and the load I will put on you is light (Mt. 11:28–29).

When I did not confess my sins,
I was worn out from crying all day long.
Day and night you punished me, Lord;
my strength was completely drained,
as moisture is dried up by the summer heat.
Then I confessed my sins to you;
I did not conceal my wrongdoings.
I decided to confess them to you,
and you forgave all my sins (Ps. 32:3–5).

When I lie down, I go to sleep in peace;
you alone, O Lord, keep me perfectly safe (Ps. 4:8).

8. My God, I don't believe

Many sincere believers lack a proper understanding of God. These people have caricatured his face. The caricature is increasingly unacceptable to today's men and women—and they are quite right to reject it because it represents the face of a false God.

Who is God for us? Is our God all-powerful in human terms or all-powerful through his loving activity in the world?

If we think of God as all-powerful in human terms, there is a danger of confusing faith with passivity: 'God does everything', 'leave it to God'. There is the greater danger of gradually constructing a religion based on slavery and fear: God's favour must be earned; avoiding punishment, particularly that of eternal damnation, depends on obedience. And worse still, we drag God into blind alleys and we blame him for unfair deaths and for all the sufferings that crush humanity.

If we think of God as all-powerful through love, then we try, step by step, to live our lives as a loving response to that love which is ceaselessly offered but never imposed. We are astonished to discover how free we are before God, responsible for our own lives, for the lives of our brothers and sisters and of the world.

The most important part of our faith is to believe that we are infinitely loved. If we accept this love, we change completely. We are 're-created', and from being servants we become free children of an 'adorable' Father. Because of love and not out of duty we do our best to gratify the Father's every wish.

My God, I don't believe
that you cause the rain to fall or the sun to shine,
   to order,
   on request,
so that the christian's corn will grow
or the parish priest's Bazaar will be a success;
that you find work for the virtuous unemployed person
   but leave others to search alone
   and never find a job;
that you protect from accidents
the child whose mother prays
   and allow the other one to be killed,

the little one who has no mother to storm heaven;
that you give us food to eat
    when we ask you for it,
    and allow people to die of hunger
    when we stop asking for your help.

My God, I don't believe
that you lead us wherever you want us to go,
    and that we only have to let ourselves be led:
that you send us hardship
    and all we can do is to accept it;
that you offer us success
    and we only have to thank you for it;
that when you make a decision,
    you know what is good for us
    and it is up to us to accept with resignation.

No, my God, I don't believe
that you are a dictator,
    all-powerful,
    imposing your will,
    for the good of your people;
that we are puppets
    and that you pull the strings
    whenever you feel like it;
that you make us play out a mysterious drama
    in which the smallest details
        have been pre-ordained by you since the beginning of
                                                      time.
No, I don't believe it,
    I no longer believe it,
because I know now, my God,
    that this is not what you want,
    that you couldn't do this,
because you are LOVE,
because you are our FATHER
    and because we are your children.
    Forgive us, oh my God,
for having distorted your image as a loving Father.
We believed that in order to know and understand you

we should imagine you
    endowed with infinite power and authority,
of the kind that we humans too often seek.
Thinking of you and speaking about you,
    we have used words that are alright in themselves,
but in our closed hearts they have turned into traps
    and we have translated:
    omnipotence,
    the will of God,
    commandment,
    obedience,
    judgment . . .
into the language of arrogant men and women
who dream of dominion over their brothers and sisters;
and we have assigned to you:
    punishment,
    suffering and death,
    while what you wish for us is
    forgiveness,
    happiness and life.
    Forgive us, oh my God,
because we haven't had the courage to believe that,
                through your love for us,
    you have always wanted us to be *free*,
free not just to say yes or no
    to what you have decided for us in advance,
    but free to reflect,
    to choose,
    to act as independent beings
    throughout our lives.

We haven't had the courage to believe
that you wanted our freedom so much
that you risked sin, allowing us the freedom to sin,
    that you risked evil,
    suffering,
    spoiled fruits of our misused freedom,
    awful consequence of our rejection of your love,
that you risked losing,
in the eyes of many of your children,

your halo of infinite goodness
and the glory of your omnipotence.

We haven't had the courage to understand
that when you wanted to reveal yourself to us definitively,
  you came on this earth,
  small,
  weak,
  naked,
and that you died on a cross,
  abandoned,
  powerless,
  naked,
to signify to the world that your only power
is the infinite power of love,
love which frees us,
  so that we can love.

I know now, my God, that you can do everything
  . . . except take our freedom away from us!

Thank you, my God, for this beautiful and frightening
                                              freedom,
  supreme gift of your infinite love.
  We are free!
  Free!
Free to harness nature, little by little,
  and to use it in the service of our sisters and brothers;
free to abuse it
  by exploiting it for our own advantage;
free to protect and develop life,
  to fight against suffering
  and sickness,
or free to squander intelligence, energy, money,
  to manufacture weapons
  and to kill each other;
free to give or not to give children to you;
free to organize the sharing of our wealth,
or to allow millions of human beings
to die of hunger on fertile land;

free to love
　　or free to hate,
free to follow you
　　or to reject you.

We are free . . .
　　but loved *infinitely*.

　　So I believe, my God,
that because you love us and because you are our Father
you have always wanted us to be happy forever,
　　that you always propose
　　but never impose.

I believe that your Spirit of love
　　at the centre of our life,
　　whispers to us, faithfully, each day,
　　the desires of your Father.
And I believe that amid the great dove-tailing
　　of human freedoms,
　　the events that touch us, all our involvements,
　　those we have chosen
　　and those we haven't chosen,
sources of joy or of cruel suffering,
　　all of these,
　　through us and for us,
with the help of your Spirit who is with us,
thanks to your love for us in your son,
thanks to our freedom to be open to your love,
　　all of these can be providential,
　　each time they become part of us.

　　Oh my great and loving God,
so humble and unobtrusive before me
　　that I cannot reach out and understand you
　　unless I become like a little child,
let me believe with all my strength
　　in your only omnipotence:
　　the omnipotence of your *love*.
Then, one day, in union with my sisters and brothers,

proud of having lived my life as a free human being,
   supremely happy,
   I will be able to hear you say:
   'Go my child, your faith has redeemed you'.

Even before the world was made, God had already chosen us to be his through our union with Christ, so that we would be holy and without fault before him. Because of his love God has already decided that through Jesus Christ he would make us his sons—this was his pleasure and purpose. Let us praise God for his glorious grace, for the free gift he gave us in his dear Son (Eph. 1:4–6).

Whoever does not love does not know God, for God is love. And God showed his love for us by sending his only Son into the world, so that we might have life through him. This is what love is: it is not that we have loved God, but that he loved us and sent his Son to be the means by which our sins are forgiven (1 Jn. 4:8–10).

9. My friend died last night, Lord . . .

It is God's will that each of his children is born, lives and dies. But we should all die a 'natural' death . . . at the end of our lives. Premature deaths resulting from accidents or illness are not God's doing, nor are they 'the will of God' any more than just a matter of luck.

Most accidents are the sad consequences of our freedom. It is only with the help of the Spirit that we can discover the extent of our own responsibility, as well as that of our brothers and sisters, in the dove-tailing of all that we do. Many 'accidents' would be avoided if we lived as Jesus asked us to live.

Many illnesses are still incurable. They remain incurable because we haven't succeeded yet in harnessing nature. This is our task as human beings. God gave us the earth to subdue and to put it at the service of humankind, and he trusts us. With certain exceptions, he doesn't take over from us by performing 'miracles'. It is the job of the researchers, doctors, etc. to continue the struggle. We cause many of our own illnesses by not using our bodies properly and by not paying attention to what they are saying to us, and all too often we devote a lot more money, intelligence and energy to inventing ways of killing each other than to finding and exploiting ways to protect life and bring it to its full potential.

Fortunately, God does not abandon us; he has come in Jesus Christ to be with us in our struggle throughout our lives. The all-powerful gift of his love is with us always and our suffering, while not a good thing in itself, can help through Jesus Christ to make us even more aware of his saving love.

My friend died last night, Lord,
   his life
   ebbing away,
fighting the cancer to the very end,
with his family and a caring medical team.

I'm not saying, Lord:
since this is what you wanted,
may your will be done;

and still less am I saying: may your holy will be done.
   But I'm telling you, very quietly . . .
   very quietly, because so many people
   will never understand,
I'm telling you, Lord, that my friend died . . .
   and you could do nothing about it;
you couldn't do what I so desperately longed for,
you couldn't do what I so foolishly hoped for.
   And I'm weeping,
   torn apart,
   shattered,
   but my heart is at peace
because, this morning, I understood a little better
   that you were weeping with me.

Yes, Lord, I understood . . .
   thanks to you,
   and thanks to my friends;
but help me to believe
   that you want life,
   not death,
   and that because you love more
you suffer more than any of us
   when you see so many of your children
   dying before their time.

   Apart from a few exceptions,
   and this is your mystery,
I understood that because of your respect and love for us
you never wanted to take our place
in the battle against illness,
   but always offered to suffer with us
   and to struggle with us.

   I understood. . .
because my friend, Lord,
instead of asking you for a miracle
asked you to give his medical team
   the strength to search
   and to struggle to the end in their efforts to find a cure.

For himself,
    he implored you to give him the courage to suffer,
to accept the two operations,
the treatments and all the experience of pain,
so that others after him
might suffer less
and even be cured some day.

    For his family and friends
        he didn't ask for the grace of resignation,
but for the grace to stand up for life,
        to respect it,
        to develop it,
and until the very end, lulled by the music he loved,
        he asked for everyone. . .
        the joy of living.

Lord, my friend didn't offer up his suffering,
because he used to say that suffering is evil
and God doesn't like suffering.
He offered his long and painful battle
        against suffering;
        this prodigious energy,
        the strength he showed,
        thanks to you, Lord,
the superabundance of love and faith he needed
        so as not to despair,
        but to believe that this life
        is restored through you,
        beyond death.

My friend, Lord,
didn't give his suffering,
        but like you,
        with you,
        oh my Saviour Jesus,
        he gave his life
        that we might live.

My friend died last night, Lord,
   and I am weeping,
   but my heart is at peace,
because my friend died last night,
   but with you,
   he gave me life.

Then God said: 'And now we will make human beings; they will be like us and resemble us. They will have power over the fish, the birds, and all animals, domestic and wild, large and small' (Gen. 1:26).

All of creation waits with eager longing for God to reveal his sons. For creation was condemned to lose its purpose, not of its own will, but because God willed it to be so. Yet there was the hope that creation itself would one day be set free from its slavery to decay and would share the glorious freedom of the children of God. For we know that up to the present time all of creation groans with pain, like the pain of childbirth (Rom. 8:19–22).

Martha said to Jesus, 'If you had been here, Lord, my brother would not have died! But I know that even now God will give you whatever you ask him for.'
'Your brother will rise to life,' Jesus told her.
'I know,' she replied, 'that he will rise to life on the last day.'
Jesus said to her, 'I am the resurrection and the life. Whoever believes in me will live, even though he dies; and whoever lives and believes in me will never die. Do you believe this?'
'Yes, Lord!' she answered. 'I do believe that you are the Messiah, the Son of God, who was to come into the world' (Jn. 11:21–26).

10. Life is before me, Lord, . . . But you are with me on the journey

Many young people are afraid of the future. They are worried particularly about their professional future and about their future family life. They don't know what paths to choose and they don't know where these paths will take them. Some become very anxious and avoid making a choice by refusing to grow up. Fear is unhealthy. It paralyses. The greatness of human beings lies in their capacity to risk life, after careful reflection, of course, but without expecting the kind of 'all risks insurance' which is not to be found.

Yes, risk-taking is dangerous; committing ourselves consciously and loyally to Jesus Christ does not save us from effort but it does guarantee peace. He wants us to be truly happy, and he wants to help us to attain this happiness regardless of the difficulties we meet on our path through life.

Life is before me, Lord,
   like an enticing fruit;
but life often frightens me,
   because if I want to gather its fruits
   I must leave home
   and start my journey;
   I must walk,
   and keep on walking,
on a road that turns and returns endlessly,
on which I can't see ahead
   the landscape of the future,
   or the hidden obstacles,
   the hands stretched out towards me
   or the faces turned away.

Setting out, Lord,
is a thrilling adventure.
I want to live. . .
but often I'm afraid.

I'm afraid of entering the huge building site, tomorrow,
where the crowds of world-builders go about their
                                    business.
  Will I find a job there?
  So many new hands are left without work
  and so many heads bursting with brains
  are waiting for employment!

I'm afraid of this mysterious world
    which fascinates and terrifies me,
    because I hear the shouts of laughter
    and I see the pleasures
    that beckon to me from afar,
but I also hear
the clamour of human suffering,
    cries which arouse my indignation,
cries that I cannot silence.

I'm afraid of this love
    which I desire with all my being,
    at the dawn of my days
    and in the depth of my nights.
Mysterious energy that inundates my heart
    and overflows my body,
and with lengthening days, importunate longing
    to encounter a face,
to recognize and be recognized
    as the one uniquely sought.
Hunger to caress it with a glance,
    to encircle it with my hands,
to taste its lips at last and let my own be tasted.
Hunger already, that this love
    may through us become flesh,
    and cry out,
    the cry of new life,
    when love bears fruit.

I desire, but at the same time I'm afraid, Lord.
So many efforts to love have miscarried before my eyes,
    illusions of happiness,

like bubbles that have burst.
So many loves are tested
    and not risked in the end.
So many couples among my friends,
    who believed they were united forever
    and then broke up their relationship so quickly!

Yes, I'm afraid, Lord,
    I dare to admit it
    and I dare to say it to you.
But if I close my eyes today
it is not because I refuse
to *see* the road ahead of me,
    but in order to find you, to pray to you,
    because I want to live, Lord,
    I want to live,
and I trust you.

Oh my God,
let me never forget to thank you for life,
    because life is yours,
    you who are the Father,
    the Father of all life,
you who have made me your child,
    your child born for *joy*.

Make me proud to be human,
    standing up straight, as men and women are called to
                                            stand,
accepting from you this marvellous vocation
    to create myself,
    to raise myself, to grow,
so as to set out rich and free
    on the road that lies ahead.

Let me welcome life
    whole-heartedly,
    firmly,
because my parents transmitted it to me through love,
    even if the love

48

perhaps
was fragile,
and I am responsible for my life
because they gave it to me.

Help me not to waste my life,
life of a body that overstretches itself,
and of a soul that is losing its way;
never to steal life from others,
but always to welcome it
when it is offered;
never to lock it up and keep it in my own heart,
instead of sharing it
with my brothers and sisters
who need it so much.

Give me the desire to seek you always,
so that I may meet you, know you and love you,
and become with you the friend you desire,
welcoming your *life* in my life,
so that my flowers and my fruit
may be yours and mine,
at the same time.

Help me to go forward,
without wanting to know
what I'm going to find
at every bend on the road,
not with my head in the clouds
but with my feet on the ground
and my hand in yours.

I'll leave home then, Lord,
confidently, joyfully
and I'll set out fearlessly on the unknown road:
the journey of life is before me
but you are travelling with me.

It is God who clothes the wild grass—grass that is here today and gone tomorrow, burnt up in the oven. Won't he be all the more sure to clothe you? How little faith you have!
So do not start worrying: 'Where will my food come from? or my drink? or my clothes?' (These are the things the pagans are always concerned about.) Your Father in heaven knows that you need all these things. Instead, be concerned above everything else with the Kingdom of God and with what he requires of you, and he will provide you with all these other things. So do not worry about tomorrow; it will have enough worries of its own. There is no need to add to the troubles each day brings (Mt. 6:30–34).

Jesus got into a boat, and his disciples went with him. Suddenly a fierce storm hit the lake, and the boat was in danger of sinking, but Jesus was asleep. The disciples went to him and woke him up. 'Save us, Lord!' they said, 'We are about to die!'
'Why are you so frightened?' Jesus answered, 'How little faith you have!' Then he got up and ordered the winds and the waves to stop, and there was a great calm (Mt. 8:23–26).

11. Lord, you were that unemployed person, the one I met an hour ago

Two thousand years ago, Jesus of Nazareth was betrayed, arrested, unjustly condemned, tortured and executed. Dying on the cross he took upon himself all our sins and all our sufferings. His 'historical' passion has been accomplished, but it still continues today in his members.

Jesus Christ continues to suffer in and through every person who suffers. In this sense, it can be said that his Way of the Cross is not yet finished.

Jesus died a victim of our sins. Because of them he was crucified. We also are victims of our sins. God doesn't 'punish' us on account of our faults. We punish ourselves, individually and collectively—and this is a fact that bears repetition.

Great problems such as the underdevelopment of peoples and the terrible suffering that goes with it, but also wars . . . unemployment, etc . . . all of these are, in one way or another, consequences of the 'collective sin' of humanity.

God does not turn stones into bread, but he does give us his Word. Strengthened by this Word, we must help the 'victims of sin' and with our brothers and sisters as well as with our Brother we must also fight to eliminate the causes of so much suffering.

Lord,
   you must be tired this evening,
because you stood in line for a long time
at the employment bureau.
   You must feel humiliated this evening,
because you heard so many hurtful remarks
during the course of the day.
   You must feel disheartened this evening,
because tomorrow . . . your unemployment benefit runs
out
   and you have no further rights:
no right to eat,
no right to feed your family,
no right to live . . .
only the right to die.

51

Lord,
how you must be suffering this evening!
Because you were that unemployed person
I met an hour ago.
It was you.
I know it was you
because you told me so in your Holy Gospel.
'I was naked,
a stranger,
sick,
in prison'
unemployed!
I know it was you,
but I forgot about it.

Lord,
your Way of the Cross is so long!
And I thought it was finished.
I thought you came to the end of it
up there on Golgotha,
after long hours of torture,
when you were about thirty years old.

I knew that you came among us,
like us,
one of ourselves,
and that you shared our journey,
faithfully taking your place
in the ranks of the suffering.
But I didn't know
that your Way of the Cross had already begun
long ago,
at the beginning of time,
when the first human beings
on the first land
met with their first sufferings.
And I didn't know that it won't end
until the last human beings
have cried out for the last time,
on the last crosses.

Lord,
even though you played your part to the bitter end,
two thousand years ago,
    faithfully,
    perfectly,
the Way of the Cross of your sisters and brothers is long,
    very long,
and with them and through them, you continue to be
    exploited,
    rejected,
    humiliated,
    imprisoned,
    stripped,
    tortured,
    crucified,
heart and body shattered,
detailing in time your own all-giving suffering
on all the crosses in the world
erected by men and women.

    You have taught me now, Lord!. . .
that those who love
experience the suffering of the people they love.
The more one loves the more one suffers,
    and since you love infinitely
you suffer infinitely when you see us suffering.
    And it is thus, Lord,
assuming all our pain,
    that you are crucified, in your members,
    until the end of time.
And this is your great Passion
of suffering and of love.

    Lord,
I wasn't there on the road to Golgotha
    two thousand years ago,
like your mother
weeping and offering,
the holy women lamenting,
the people in the crowd who were silenced by fear,

the others shouting their hatred,
and Simon of Cyrene forced
   to help you.
But I'm there today and I see you
   when I see men and women suffering,
   I speak to you when I speak to them,
and I help you to carry your cross
when I help them to carry theirs.

   Lord,
   I want to be Simon of Cyrene
on the Way of the Cross of today's men and women.
What's the point of weeping over you
who died two thousand years ago,
   if I don't suffer with my brothers and sisters
   who are suffering today?
What use is it to meditate
   and moan during pious ceremonies
   if I don't see you every day
   toiling along my road?

   But as I pray this evening,
   before them,
   before you,
I'm thinking also that the crosses of humanity
don't assemble themselves.
We manufacture them,
   every day,
   through our selfishness,
   our pride,
and through the long array of our many sins.

We are cross-makers!
   Artisans, self-employed
   or working together,
   perfectly organized manufacturers,
   we produce crosses on an assembly line,
   more and more,
   better and better:
   crosses for broken homes,

crosses for abandoned children,
crosses for people starving to death,
crosses for combatants on the battle field,
crosses for . . . the unemployed.
And crosses . . .
and crosses,
of every shape and size!
And if we are to be Simon of Cyrene, Lord,
for our suffering brothers and sisters,
we must struggle,
all of us together,
to dismantle the innumerable factories where crosses are
made.

Thank you, Lord,
because it was you,
you were that unemployed person
I met an hour ago,
and it is you,
speaking to me today,
through the unemployed.

When the Son of Man comes as King and all the angels with him, he will sit on his royal throne, and the people of all the nations will be gathered before him. Then he will divide them into two groups, just as a shepherd separates the sheep from the goats. He will put the righteous people on his right and the others on his left. Then the King will say to the people on his right, 'Come, you that are blessed by my Father! Come and possess the kingdom which has been prepared for you ever since the creation of the world. I was hungry and you fed me, thirsty and you gave me a drink; I was a stranger and you received me in your homes, naked and you clothed me; I was sick and you took care of me, in prison and you visited me.' The righteous will then answer him, 'When, Lord, did we ever see you hungry and feed you, or thirsty and give you a drink? When did we ever see you a stranger and welcome you in our homes, or naked and clothe you?' The King will reply,'I tell you, whenever you did this for one of the least important of these brothers of mine, you did it for me!' (Mt. 25:31–40)

At all times we carry in our mortal bodies the death of Jesus, so that his life also may be seen in our bodies (2 Cor. 4:10).

Help to carry one another's burdens, and in this way you will obey the law of Christ (Gal. 6:2).

12. Prayer from the depths of my solitude

God is 'subsisting relationship', Father, Son and Holy Spirit, so united that they are one. Human beings, male and female, created in the image of God, also exist in 'relationships' but they are not complete and perfect. They must create themselves gradually in relationships of understanding, respect and love with all other human beings and particularly with those close to them.

However, one of the great dramas in today's world is the breakdown of human relationships. People are crowded into towns, apartment buildings, blocks of flats, public transport . . . but often live beside each other without ever really knowing each other. This is why so many people are lonely, especially in certain categories such as the elderly, the sick, the handicapped, and prisoners. . . . This is very serious, because if men and women have no relationships with others they slowly destroy themselves and can die from loneliness.

People waiting for somebody to join them 'in the depths of their solitude' may have to wait for a long time. The only way they can overcome their solitude is by coming out of themselves and going towards others. Jesus Christ is with them, Jesus who came so that all humanity might be made into one body in him.

I'm alone,
alone, Lord, do you understand?
　　Alone
　　And there's a party going on outside.

I turned off the radio,
which so often creates the illusion of a presence,
　　but suddenly
　　silence filled the room
and anguish sneaked into my heart
　　and stayed there.

For a moment I listened
　　to some noises on the stairs.
I imagined that I heard footsteps . . .

somebody coming up?
    What's the point of this foolish hope,
    since I'm not expecting anyone
    . . . and nobody will come!

Lord, if you wanted to,
you would send me somebody!
    I need somebody,
I need a hand, Lord,
    only a hand on my hand,
    resting there like a bird;
I need lips on my forehead
    and the warmth of a kiss;
a glance,
    just a glance
    to prove to me
that at least I exist for someone;
a few words,
    and in these words
    a person caring for me.

    But nobody will come.
    I'm alone.
    Alone.
    And there's a party going on outside.

Yes, you can speak, Lord,
and I'm really listening!
But I've heard it all before,
    and the priests have told me the same thing:
'You are not alone' because 'I am there.'
Yes, you are there,
    but without lips,
    without a glance towards me and without words.
And I'm not an angel,
    since you gave me a body!

Have you nothing else to say, Lord?
    Do you not speak either?
    Are you angry?. . .

I have been a prisoner in my loneliness for a long time,
    and crossword puzzles
    on their squares
    can't be turned into a door
    through which I can escape
from my undeserved imprisonment.

But all of a sudden I think,
or perhaps it is you speaking to me again,
    I think that I'm not the only one
    languishing in solitude.
    I know some of them live near me,
    and I know this harsh world
where millions of people,
bodies are crowded together,
in apartment buildings or in the crowd,
    living beside each other,
    rubbing shoulders,
    knocking against each other,
    without ever meeting each other.
This is not what you wanted, Lord,
you who said that you came
to gather your scattered children
    and to make them into one family.

Now, Lord, my suffering
tells me a lot about the suffering of others,
and I hear their cries
which are louder than my own,
and I understand at last
    that there is only one remedy
    that can heal my solitude:
    it is to reach out to others
    and heal their loneliness.

I've found my vocation, Lord!
I who so often felt useless,
    and capable of so little,
    despite my anxiety to be helpful:
I'll be a maker and mender in the Church.

I'll try to tighten links which were loose,
    and perhaps renew
    some which were broken.
I'll repair a little of the fabric of the family,
and since on this earth, Lord, you no longer have
    hands, lips,
    glances and words,
I offer myself as sub-contractor,
    for all those whose need, like mine,
    is for a body,
    even an ageing body,
to tell them that they are not alone
and that Somebody loves them.

    Goodbye loneliness!
It's late this evening, Lord, but I promise you
    that tomorrow
I'll begin my work
by going to visit my neighbour.
    Good night, Lord . . .
    bereft of kisses,
    once again
    I have nothing to return,
but tomorrow I'll be ready with a kiss
    and I'll be able to give it.

*Then Jesus went with his disciples to a place called Gethsemane,
and he said to them, 'Sit here while I go over there and pray.' He
took with him Peter and the two sons of Zebedee. Grief and
anguish came over him, and he said to them,'The sorrow in my
heart is so great that it almost crushes me. Stay here and keep
watch with me.'*
*He went a little farther on, threw himself face downwards on the
ground, and prayed, 'My father, if it is possible, take this cup of
suffering from me! Yet not what I want, but what you want.'
Then he returned to the three disciples and found them asleep;
and he said to Peter, 'How is it that you three were not able to
keep watch with me even for one hour?' (Mt. 26:36–40)*

Dear Friends, if this is how God loved us, then we should love one another. No one has ever seen God, but if we love one another, God lives in union with us, and his love is made perfect in us (1 Jn. 4:11–12).

13. Life is good, Lord, and today is Easter Sunday

Jesus told his disciples that they must take up their crosses and follow him. But they must follow him to the very end. Now Jesus did not stop either at Golgotha or at the tomb. We believe that he is alive, that he is risen. Drawn with him into his death—our death to sin—we rise with him, alive with the new life which is his.

In a certain sense the passion of Jesus Christ was not completed, since he continues to suffer and die each day in his members. In the same way, one can say that the resurrection was not completed. Easter is not only something that happened in the past—the greatest event in history. When, in Jesus Christ, we assume the passage from the death of sin to the life he offers us, then it is Easter every day.

Of course, not every human passage from death to life automatically implies entry to the Kingdom, but it is a mystery of creation that develops in Christ, 'For through him God created everything . . . God created the whole universe through him and for him. Christ existed before all things, and in union with him all things have their proper place' (Col. 1:16–17).

Each person grows and develops each day in Christ, rises from the dead each day in him, and will rise until the end of time.

Life is good, Lord,
  and I want to grasp it
as one plucks flowers on a spring morning.
  But I know, Lord,
  that the flowers appear
only at the end of a long and harsh winter.

Forgive me, Lord,
for not believing firmly enough in life's spring–time.
Too often, life seems like a long winter,
  endlessly weeping
  over its dead leaves
  and its vanished flowers.

And yet, I believe in you, Lord,
    with all my strength,
But I come up against your tomb and find it empty.

And when the apostles of today tell me
    that they have seen you alive,
I'm like Thomas,
    I need to see and to touch.
    I beg you, Lord,
    to give me sufficient faith
to hope for spring in the depths of winter,
    to believe in the triumph of Easter
    over Good Friday.

    Because you have risen, Lord,
    you are *alive!*
    You, the older brother,
always united with all of us,
    you, who loved us so much
that us you became flesh,
bringing us with you into death to sin,
    the real death.
    You, our 'head',
first-born of the womb of the earth,
    first human born in heaven,
now you draw all your brothers and sisters
    forward with you, one by one,
    the 'members' of your body,
until the whole of humanity, re–united at last,
    is inserted by you,
    with you,
    in you,
    into the Holy Trinity.

    Lord, you are risen!
Because of you LIFE has emerged
    triumphant from the tomb.
From now on, the spring will never dry up,
    new life offered to all,

to re-create us forever,
children of a God who is waiting for us,
so that every day may be Easter
and *joy eternal.*

Yesterday was Easter Sunday, Lord,
  but it's Easter today.
Whenever we are prepared to die to ourselves,
with you we open up
  the tomb of our hearts,
allowing the spring to gush and your life to flow.
  And even though so many men and women
    don't know, alas,
    that you are there already
    in our human efforts,
they'll discover this later on, in the light of your presence.

Yesterday was Easter Sunday,
  but it's Easter today:
when children share their sweets
  after a secret struggle
  not to keep the lot for themselves;
when husband and wife kiss each other
  after a slight argument or a painful disagreement;
when adversaries sign a truly just agreement
  after a long battle;
when researchers discover the saving remedy,
  and the person who would have died without medical
                                                help
  is brought back to life;
when prison doors open
  at the end of the sentence,
  and the prisoner in the cell
  is already sharing cigarettes with companions;
when someone finally finds work
  and is able to bring home a little money;
when the newspaper announces that the important
                              Conference
  has done something to solve the problems of the world.

Every day is Easter,
thousands and thousands of Easters,
but I don't really know, Lord,
   how to look around me
   and see more spring flowers
   than dead leaves.

As I pray to you this evening, Lord,
I don't want to
   go on complaining,
   weeping for my sins
   and for the sins of the world,
   sins which brought you to the tomb
   and which breed death for us.
I don't want to spend the time imploring your forgiveness
   for locking away so much,
   for burying so much,
   and as a result, losing hope in life too often.

I won't camp out with you this evening, Lord,
in the garden of olives,
   to wake up tomorrow morning
   with a head like Good Friday.
I'm frequently exasperated
by too many easy Alleluias,
but my only prayer this evening
will be a heart-felt thanksgiving,
   for the lifted stones,
   the emergence from the tomb,
   and for this New Life
   gushing beneath my feet, today

   Yes, Lord, life is good,
   because it is your Father who made it good.
   Life is good,
because it is you who gave it back to us
when we had lost it.
   Life is good,
because it is your own life offered for us . . .
   But it is our responsibility to make it flourish,

and if I want to offer it to you each evening
then I must gather it on the pathways of men and
                                                    women,
just as children out walking
pluck wild flowers
to make bouquets
to offer to their parents.

Life is good, Lord,
it was Easter today.

It was late that Sunday evening, and the disciples were gathered together behind locked doors, because they were afraid of the Jewish authorities. Then Jesus came and stood among them. 'Peace be with you.' he said. After saying this, he showed them his hands and his side. The disciples were filled with joy at seeing the Lord. Jesus said to them again, 'Peace be with you. As the Father sent me, so I send you' (Jn. 20:19–21).

Since you have accepted Christ Jesus as Lord, live in union with him. Keep your roots deep in him, build your lives on him, and become stronger in your faith, as you were taught. And be filled with thanksgiving . . .
For the full content of divine nature lives in Christ . . . For when you were baptized, you were buried with Christ, and in baptism you were also raised with Christ through your faith in the active power of God, who raised him from death (Col. 2:6–7; 9–12).

You have been raised to life with Christ, so set your hearts on the things that are in heaven, where Christ sits on his throne at the right-hand side of God (Col. 3:1).

14. My friends said: 'Will you come and have a drink?'

Human beings need to come together. Through various gestures, they take on the risk of an encounter. Having a drink together is one of the most usual ways of doing this. Hidden behind the search for friendship is a thirst that is something more than the search for justifiable personal satisfaction, for a satisfaction that is also human. Men and women need God and they thirst for the water which will refresh their hearts. Jesus Christ offers us 'living water', his life, which will flow for us and our brothers and sisters until the end of time. We should go to drink at this well more often.

My friends said:
'Will you come and have a drink?'
And I thought about the innumerable invitations,
    repeated every day:
'You'll have something to drink?'
'What will you have?'
'Come on, we'll drink to my birthday!'
'An now. . . let's drink to us!'
    drink and drink again . . .
    Lord,
    are people always thirsty, then?

I know they are thirsty.
Their bodies are thirsty sometimes, perhaps,
    but above all, their hearts.
    Lonely people looking for company,
    for words to hear,
    for gales of laughter to drown their sorrows,
    for an exchange of glances
    of amusement or complicity,
    for gestures which touch them,
to know that they exist,
and that they are recognized,
to experience,
to feel,

67

that through this network of relationships
    established in a moment,
    there is a little bit of life
    which engenders warmth and unity.

They are thirsty,
they feel like drinking,
    but their thirst is not quenched.
Tomorrow, they'll begin all over again.

I'm thirsty too, Lord,
    thirsty for shared life.
But I know that there is another thirst,
    hidden beneath my human thirsts,
    the thirst for your *life* in my life.
I search for you, Lord,
    but all too often
I look for you far away,
    while you are waiting for me, close by,
    . . . so close that I don't see you.
And yet, you have said to me:
    'Whoever loves me will obey my teaching.
    My Father will love him,
    and my Father and I
    will come to him
    and live with him.' (Jn. 14:23)

Then why, Lord,
why do I walk so often
    alone in my barren desert,
    with withered limbs
    and empty hands,
why do I live without life
    when you offer me yours?

I beg you, Lord,
    that I may hear more often
your silent invitations
over the noise of my days.
Because you also, Lord,

offer me a drink!
You offer me water
Which will quench my thirst forever.

And since you are waiting for me at the threshold of my
heart,
as you waited for the Samaritan woman long ago, beside
Jacob's well,
let me plunge often,
very often,
into the deepest part of myself,
and find the well,
and drink from this well
which never runs dry.

Then my thirst will be quenched, Lord,
I will be renewed,
my troubles overcome,
and my words and gestures purified.
And I will be able to turn towards my brothers and sisters
again,
to have a drink with them.
I won't be going reluctantly,
grudging the time lost,
but whole-heartedly,
thirst quenched and heart alive with your *life*.
I too will contribute
my words,
my laughter,
my glances and gestures,
and if my friends say when they are leaving:
'Thanks a million,
we've had a great time together,'
I'll offer these thanks to you, Lord,
because through me, thanks to YOU,
perhaps they will have tasted
a few mouthfuls of your *living water*.

Jesus answered the Samaritan women,'Whoever drinks this water will be thirsty again, but whoever drinks the water that I will give him will never be thirsty again. The water that I will give him will become in him a spring which will provide him with life-giving water and give him eternal life' (Jn. 4:13–14).

Two days later there was a wedding in the town of Cana in Galilee. Jesus' mother was there, and Jesus had also been invited to the wedding. When the wine had given out, Jesus' mother said to him, 'They have no wine left.' 'You must not tell me what to do,' Jesus replied. 'My time has not yet come.' Jesus' mother then told the servants, 'Do whatever he tells you.'
The Jews have rules about ritual washing, and for this purpose six stone water jars were there, each one large enough to hold about a hundred litres. Jesus told the servants, 'Fill these jars with water.' They filled them to the brim, and he told them, 'Now draw some water out and take it to the man in charge of the feast.' They took him the water, which now had turned into wine, and he tasted it. He did not know where this wine had come from (but, of course, the servants who had drawn out the water knew) (Jn. 2:1–9).

15. Lord, I'm afraid for human beings, they're growing up too fast

We are proud of today's wonderful scientific and technical discoveries, but we tremble sometimes before the constantly increasing power of the scientists. Where are we going? Perhaps humankind is becoming a sorcerer's apprentice, manipulating the universe and life itself, and will finish by destroying itself?

Nevertheless, it is the beautiful and exciting vocation of men and women to continue the creation of the world and of humanity. God gave them this task from the beginning. They are not 'creatures' but 'co-creators' with Jesus Christ, through whom all things were made and without whom nothing was made.

Some time ago, the French philosopher Henri Bergson claimed that our modern world needs more soul, but as men and women grow and become responsible it also needs more love in Christ Jesus.

Once again, Lord,
as I turn on my radio,
I hear that for the first time
    human beings are achieving
one of those marvels
    that nobody previously imagined
    would one day become possible.
And I no longer know, Lord,
    if I should admire the power of men and women,
    or tremble before it,
    or even condemn it, occasionally.

They have discovered and harnessed
the prodigious energy hidden in matter;
they launch hundreds of satellites into space,
    they explore the planets
    and prepare to occupy them.
They invent and manufacture instruments
    which calculate
    and do in a few minutes
    what it would take a thousand human brains
    a thousand hours to accomplish.

They graft new organs
onto failing bodies.
They produce babies in test-tubes,
    and before long they will be capable
    of moulding these babies' faces according to taste.
They keep life on stand-by
and make it bloom,
when they decide
and as they wish.
They create . . . and they continue creating . . .
and will create still more . . .
and we discover to our astonishment
    that human beings succeed in doing
    what we thought
    only God could do,
    and what we were still requesting, yesterday,
    in unavailing prayers.

Have men and women grown up so much,
    Lord,
    and is their power so great
that they will take your place from now on,
    and relegate you to heaven . . .
    a heaven that is becoming more distant every day?
Are men and women gods,
    unaware of it until now,
    but finally discovering their true identity
as they grow up?

This is what some people think and say,
    and I can't believe it,
    but I'm afraid for human beings,
    they're growing up too fast!
And, nevertheless, I believe.

I believe that none of the world's scientists,
    regardless of the machines they have,
    or their calculations,
    or the calculation of their machines,
will discover where the train of life comes from,

where it is going,
who the passengers are,
and for what mysterious purpose they have boarded
    the train.

I believe also, Lord,
    that like all of us,
    the greatest scientists
search for someone who loves them
    and whom they can love,
because some day they may succeed in making us live,
much better and much longer,
    without bread,
    without water,
but they'll never be able to produce a human being
    who can attain full development without love,
    . . . and love
is something they will never manufacture.

I believe that the greatest scientists,
    like all of us,
    weep when their children die,
    even if they have been able to postpone the death for a
                               long time.
And I believe that they also search during the night,
    trying to discover
    if something of the dead child is alive somewhere.
. . . But none of their colleagues will ever tell them,
    because they don't know,
    and their science will never teach them.

What will we do tomorrow, Lord,
    if men and women distance themselves from you,
    so arrogantly,
    and . . . lose sight of you?
What will we do if increasing numbers of them
    end up believing that you are useless
. . . while others are convinced that you don't exist?
Who will teach us the truth about ourselves,
    if not you,

73

who said:
I am the truth . . .
the light of the world . . .
whoever follows me
will never walk in darkness.[1]
   Who will be able to receive this,
   since you also told us
   that it will never be
the conquest of science and scientists,
   but accessible only to those
   who are poor of heart.[2]

If men and women have grown so big,
how will they be able to go down on their knees
   to welcome this truth
   in the dark night of faith?

Yes Lord, I'm afraid for human beings,
because they're growing up too fast.
My child, says the Lord,
science is not a bad thing.
You mustn't be afraid to search
   and to discover the secrets of matter
   and of life.
It is the glory of the Father to see you growing up.
It is your duty as a human being to do everything,
   so that all of you may be raised up.
   But never forget that your intellect
   will always remain limited,
   even if it is prodigiously developed.
Only your heart can open itself to the infinite,
   while opening itself to my *life*,
And only my *life* can enable you to become,
   not like gods,
   but true children of God.[3]

1. Jn. 8:12.
2. Mt.11:25.
3. Gen. 3:3–5.

Don't be afraid of the power of human beings,
    developing so stupendously.
The Father of heaven
    is not jealous of the greatness of his children.
    He made men and women to be creators,
    and since the beginning of time
    has wished to share his power with them.

You see, it's not their power
    that you should fear,
but what they do and will do with their power as it
                                        increases.

    Because if their minds
    are enriched by knowledge,
    and their hearts
    are not still more enriched by my love,
they will build Towers of Babel, again,
    to reach up to the sky.[4]
    The towers will collapse,
    and then they will kill each other.

My child, you are afraid for your brothers and sisters.
    Are you afraid of the suffering
    that results from human pride?
I understand you,
    I was a victim of it myself,
    but I carried this suffering.
Have no doubt about the final victory,
because I overcame the world.

*Of course some of them preach Christ because they are jealous
and quarrelsome, but others from genuine goodwill. These do so
from love, because they know that God has given me the work of
defending the gospel. The others do not proclaim Christ sincerely,
but from a spirit of selfish ambition; they think that they will
make more trouble for me while I am in prison (Phil. 1:15–17).*

4. Gen. 11:4–8.

75

All of creation waits with eager longing for God to reveal his sons. For creation was condemned to lose its purpose, not of its own will, but because God willed it to be so. yet there was the hope that creation itself would one day be set free from its slavery to decay and would share the glorious freedom of the children of God. For we know that up to the present time all of creation groans with pain, like the pain of childbirth (Rom. 8:19–22).

16. I'm a long way, Lord, from giving you the place you should have in my life

We believe sincerely that if people want to build the world and develop humanity without God, they are risking catastrophe. But what place do we give God in our lives? Is Jesus Christ the one who gives meaning to our existence? Can we say honestly that the Gospel throws light on our daily existence? And as for the time we offer to the Lord, isn't it just whatever time we have left over—if we have any left over—after fulfilling all our obligations? And when we are bringing up our children, what priority do we choose for their lives? Wouldn't it be a good idea if, from time to time, we took a critical look at our own lives in the presence of the Lord, so as to hear him saying to us: 'Will a person gain anything if he wins the whole world and loses his life?' (Mt. 16.26)

I've told you, Lord:
   I'm afraid that human beings,
becoming omnipotent through science,
   will finish by forgetting you,
and will gradually destroy themselves
by doing without you.[1]
   But it occurs to me today,
   that I'm a long way from giving you
   the place that you ought to have
   in my own life.

I take the time to educate myself,
   to inform myself,
   because I regret sometimes
   that I don't know more.
I read books,
   some of them serious . . .
   and others that are less serious.
I skim through newspapers and magazines.

1. Cf. 'Lord, I'm afraid for human beings, they're growing up too fast!' p. 71

I listen to the radio,
I watch television . . .

   I have good reasons for all this.
One must keep up to date,
one must stay on top in this demanding world . . . !
   It has to be done, if one is to live,
   and if one's family is to live!
   And I find the time,
   I take plenty of time,
out of the time I have for living.

But for you, Lord?
   to be up to date about you,
   to be more in touch with you?
You come later, Lord. . . afterwards,
   . . . when I have some time to spare!

And my children, Lord . . .?
I want them to be successful in life,
   but what kind of success?
First of all, they must learn
   as much as, or more than
   I've learned.
   I ask this of them,
   demand it of them . . .
   and sometimes punish them.
I fix priorities for them:
   this year you must move up to the next class,
   this year you have your exam.
   I have nothing against
   your youth movement,
   your formation week-end,
   your retreat . . .
   But . . . later on.

This is how I live in reality, Lord,
   and how I behave with my children.
And I'm alarmed by the hypocritical gap,
   between what I think,

and what I say,
and how I live.

Lord,
you who came before us
    to reveal the secret of life to us,
    and the path of love which leads to happiness,
place deep within us the desire to meet you
in order to know you better,
    and the hunger to know you better
    in order to follow and serve you better.
Make us seekers for God,
    not only through our intelligence
    but also through our hearts.
Help us to find the time for you,
    not only time snatched
    from the usual futilities,
    but fresh time,
    new time,
like that which the lover suddenly finds
    for a love which appears unexpectedly
    in a life that is full already.

Lord, grant
to us parents,
    who gave life to our children
    even though they didn't ask to be born,
the ambition first of all to make them understand
that life is not a gift
to be used only for their pleasure,
    but a treasure which must bear fruit
    so that it can be given to others.
Help us to pass on to them a taste for study,
not so that they may succeed
    in gaining more power
    and earning more money,
but because they are responsible before God
for the gifts they have received.
    and because they must develop them,

so that tomorrow
they may be better able to serve others.

Give us enough true faith
   to enable them to discover
   that religion is not a lesson
   to be learned and to know by heart,
   a rule to be followed
   in order to live more comfortably,
but Somebody to meet,
to know,
to love.

Help us, Lord,
   because if we teach them false reasons for living
   we'll be sending them down blind alleys.
They may succeed, perhaps,
in collecting a few deceptive pleasures,
but they will never find true *happiness* there,
the happiness for which they were made.

Help us, Lord,
   you who have said to us:
   what use is it
   if you gain the whole world and lose your life? [2]
   And what use is it if we help our children
   to conquer the world
   and lose their lives?

Then Jesus told them this parable: There was once a rich man who had land which bore good crops. He began to think to himself, 'I haven't anywhere to keep all my crops. What can I do? This is what I will do,' he told himself; 'I will tear down my barns and build bigger ones, where I will store my corn and all my other goods. Then I will say to myself, Lucky man! You have all the good things you need for many years. Take life easy, eat, drink and enjoy yourself!' And Jesus concluded, 'This is how it is with those who pile up riches for themselves but are not rich in God's sight' (Lk. 12:16–21).

2. Mt. 16:26.

80

You are like salt for all mankind. But if salt loses its saltiness, there is no way to make it salty again. It has become worthless, so it is thrown out and people trample on it (Mt. 5:13).

17. *Last night, Lord, I didn't turn off the kitchen tap properly*

A life marked by brilliant activity and lived in the public eye is not necessarily a complete existence. On the contrary, as St Thérèse (the Little Flower) and others have shown us, a life made up of the smallest things and lived in the shadows can lead to holiness and radiate to the ends of the earth. The Church made little Thérèse patron saint of the missions.

Often, we find it a considerable effort not to dream of doing extraordinary things while forgetting to do what we have to do, conscientiously. Dreaming about one's life is not the way to live it. Provided we are open to him, it is God who gives our existence its infinite dimension.

Last night, Lord,
I didn't turn off the kitchen tap properly.
　　The drop of water doesn't matter,
　　the little drop,
　　so tiny,
　　which dripped continuously into the sink.
What can one do with a little drop of water?

But this morning I found the sink full,
　　it had been overflowing all night.

You know, Lord, that I'm often driven to despair
by the things repeated a thousand times in my daily life.
So many little things to do,
　　in the house,
　　at work,
　　in my commitments,
little things that seem unimportant,
　　useless,
compared with all that needs to be done,
compared with what is done by important people
　　who are written about in the newspapers
　　and shown on television
　　because they do great things.

Since you invite me, Lord,
through the experiences of every day,
   just to live a quiet life,
   where I am,
   help me to be faithful,
like Mary your mother, who did great things
by doing very small things
very well every day.
And I'll fill my life
with thousands of drops of water,
   full to the brim.
My life will be fertile,
because it will flow even during the night—
   in the night of my days,
   as in the night of my nights.
It will overflow
from a heart which doesn't want to hold it back.
And the dry lands
around me will bloom again,
and my thirsty neighbours
will drink from my cup,
   because through you, Lord,
   the drops of my life
   will become a river of *living water*.

Jesus went on to say, 'The Kingdom of God is like this. A man scatters seed in his field. He sleeps at night, is up and about during the day, and all the while the seeds are sprouting and growing. Yet he does not know how it happens. The soil itself makes the plants grow and bear fruit; first the tender stalk appears, then the ear, and finally the ear full of corn. When the corn is ripe, the man starts cutting it with his sickle, because harvest time has come' (Mk. 4:26–29).

A Samaritan woman came to draw some water, and Jesus said to her, 'Give me a drink of water.' (His disciples had gone into town to buy food.) The woman answered, 'You are a Jew, and I am a Samaritan—so how can you ask me for a drink?' (Jews will not use the same cups and bowls that Samaritans use.) Jesus answered, 'If only you knew what God gives and who it is that is asking you for a drink, you would ask him, and he would give you life-giving water.'

'Sir', the woman said, 'you haven't got a bucket, and the well is deep, Where would you get the life-giving water? It was our ancestor Jacob who gave us this well; he and his sons and his flocks all drank from it. You don't claim to be greater than Jacob, do you?'

Jesus answered, 'Whoever drinks this water will be thirsty again, but whoever drinks the water that I will give him will never be thirsty again. The water that I will give him will become in him a spring which will provide him with life-giving water and give him eternal life (Jn. 4:7–14).

18. Lord, I have contemplated the faces of men and women at length

Men and women are body and spirit, in one. We believe that God created us 'in his image and likeness'. Thus, it is whole human beings, body and soul, who are the images of God, and especially their faces, mysterious shop windows that display their innermost depths.

God spoke in the Old Testament, but nobody has ever seen God.[1] Then one day, God took on a face. A face like ours, moulded from the same clay. In a certain sense, we can say from this point onwards, that if God created us 'in his image and likeness', he himself, in his son Jesus, was created 'in the image and likeness' of men and women.

And another thing: through his love Jesus Christ has incorporated all human beings in himself. As St Paul says: we have become members of his body. He gave us his life in our life, and we mustn't forget that our life is our souls and bodies together. We are brothers and sisters of Jesus Christ. We are members of the same family. It's not surprising, therefore, that we resemble each other. Jesus was a Jew, and it is not because of any particular features that we are like each other, but because of the family resemblance, that mysterious light that produces true beauty. We must develop this resemblance, in ourselves, in our brothers and sisters, by being increasingly open, through Jesus, to the life of God our Father. Then we will change from being people with anonymous—and sometimes even ill-formed—faces to people with transfigured faces and eventually with resurrection faces.

The fact remains that from now on, the only face that Jesus has on this earth is ours and that of our brothers and sisters.

Lord, I have contemplated the faces of men and women
for a long time,
    and the eyes in the faces,
    and the look in the eyes,
speaking a language more profound than gestures and
                             words.

1. Jn. 1:18

I turn back towards you, dazzled and overjoyed,
     but always more eager.

     Faces,
open books in which I have learned so much,
received so much from my brothers and sisters,
     my food,
     my nourishment,
unique faces, works of art,
     which no make-up,
     no faults,
     no wounds,
could deform permanently,
in the eyes of those who know how to look.
From what mysterious dough were you formed,
so that the breezes as well as the storms,
     the sunshine as well as the showers,
     of lives lived in the open air,
     and also of very secret lives,
     are etched in your wrinkles?

Lord, I have admired
the architecture of faces,
     cathedrals,
     chapels,
     or unobtrusive oratories,
and through the architecture I have known the riches
     and the poverty of the artist
     who fashioned them,
     from the inside,
     from every one of his thoughts,
     and from every one of his actions.

I have suffered terribly in the presence of faces that are
                              damaged, deformed,
measuring the depth of sufferings that are hidden,
     like pain that sneaks up
     from nowhere.
I have seen some of these lost faces,
     adrift,

86

drenched by thunder showers,
while on others, alas,
I've been able to gather
    only a few tears
    that have escaped from the torrents locked away.

I've drunk long draughts
of the light from faces inhabited by the sun,
    and my thirst has been quenched.
But I've waited a long time,
waited like one who watches for daybreak,
to see a smile on faces of night.
I've travelled the furrows
    on old faces,
    avenues or crevasses,
rediscovered traces
    of the joys and sorrows
that have ploughed the earth of long human lives,
    and I turn back towards you,
    dazzled and overjoyed,
    but always eager.

    Why, Lord . . .
    Why am I so fascinated?
And why have I undertaken
these long pilgrimages
to the sanctuary of faces, so often?

I admit, Lord,
    that I began out of curiosity.
Books reveal so little about the mysteries of life;
    one must look further afield
    if one is to find the light.

I thought I might turn up hidden treasure
in this clay from which we are moulded,
    dust,
    living earth,
    inhabited;
    earth and spirit mingled,

to the point where one no longer knows
where the earth is,
where the spirit is,
in these bodies, these faces,
so closely wedded to each other.

I was searching for *life*, Lord,
beyond the harmony of forms and colours.
I was searching for the 'person'
beyond all the personalities,
and beyond the persons I sought.
. . . oh, unspeakable mystery!
    I was searching . . .
    and suddenly I found
that my hunger for faces was a hunger for God.
    . . . I was searching for you, Lord,
    and you were beckoning to me!

    Lord, is it possible
that some believers
are still losing their way
even though they really want to meet you,
    and walking with their eyes in the clouds,
    unaware that they could see you every day
    when they meet their sisters and brothers on the road,
    because since you came among us,
    God, moulded from the same clay as ourselves,
God, who took on a *face*, in Jesus our brother,
    nobody can meet other men and women
    without discovering something of you in them.

You, the child of Bethlehem,
    in the faces of smiling babies . . .
You, the chastiser of the Temple,
    in the faces of adolescents
    who don't know
    whether they are children or grownups.
You, the one tempted in the desert,
    in the faces of people who are tormented,
    divided,

torn apart,
   by the evil always on offer.
You, transfigured,
   in the faces of men and women at prayer.
You, condemned and disfigured,
   in the faces of the tortured,
   groaning under blows,
   blows to the body,
   blows to the heart.
You, risen from the dead,
   in the faces of those in whom love shines
   and has made its home,
   as they sing the Easter Alleluia.

Lord,
   I want to keep going
on this unfinished pilgrimage,
seeking the faces of my brothers and sisters,
until that joyous day
when all will be in your *light* at last,
   and as I contemplate them I will be contemplating you.
But if I am to recognize you more easily
in the faces of my brothers and sisters,
   I must keep on travelling
   the long, hard road,
   with you.

Help me, Lord,
to respect the faces,
   and never to de-face them
   by trying to seize
   fleeting beauties, for myself,
or to gather from the surface of their living flesh
fruits that are ripening for others.

Let me never shut my eyes
   to faces of a different colour,
   to faces that are dark or repellent to me.
Let me never lose hope in my heart,
and let me never condemn,

when pride,
egoism or hatred,
have turned some faces
into grimacing masks for carnivals of death.

Give me the courage, Lord,
to search beneath the surface of the faces,
and not to settle on attractive river banks
or in sad unknown territory,
but on my pilgrimage to what lies beyond,
crossing over the frontiers of the visible,
let me return
to the bright Source of Light,
there in the calm lake of the heart,
where your image slowly takes shape.

Above all, Lord,
Let me look at faces
as you looked at them,
long ago,
when Scripture said of you:
he looked at him and he loved him.

Give me, Lord,
a little of your infinite tenderness,
only a little, I implore you.
Then, when I look at faces,
my gaze will be a warm caress.

Give me, Lord,
a little of your purity.
Then, when I look at faces,
my gaze will be like sapphire on wax,
I'll release songs that have been hidden away for a long
time,
and I'll make long buried agonies cry out,
and tears will flow,
smiles will radiate,
and I,
I'll listen to people singing or weeping,

and, ineffable mystery,
I'll hear you, Lord,
inviting me to sing or weep
with them,
with you, Lord.

Then God said.'And now we will make human beings; they will be like us and resemble us' . . . So God created human beings, making them to be like himself. He created them male and female . . . (Gen. 1:26–27).

Christ is the visible likeness of the invisible God. He is the first-born Son, superior to all created things (Col. 1:15–16).

The eyes are like a lamp for the body. If your eyes are sound, your whole body will be full of light; but if your eyes are no good, your body will be in darkness. So if the light in you is darkness, how terribly dark it will be! (Mt. 6:15–16).

As Jesus was starting on his way again, a man ran up, knelt before him, and asked him, 'Good teacher, what must I do to receive eternal life?'. . . Jesus looked straight at him with love and said,'You need only one thing. Go and sell all that you have and give the money to the poor, and you will have riches in heaven; then come and follow me' (Mk. 10:17, 21).

19. Lord, make me laugh!

*Many people think that laughing in church shows a lack of
respect. On the other hand, they think that crying is alright, and
in fact quite appropriate. Why one and not the other?*
*The noisy distractions and nervous laughter which are so often
nothing more than vain attempts to escape from one's self, from
others and from the harshness of daily life, are not to be confused
with the joy that is expressed in bursts of healthy laughter.*
Shouldn't one occasionally express the joy of being a christian?
*All too often, we present serious, worried faces to our brothers
and sisters. Young people complain that our Eucharists are sad
affairs. They are often bored. They're quite right to be bored!*
*It's not always easy to be joyful. Is it even possible on earth? But
it is not impossible to welcome certain moments of happiness
whole-heartedly and to share them with others.*
*If you want to hear a clear laugh exploding like fireworks at a
celebration, you should be in a convent when the nuns are at
recreation . . . look at the faces and listen.*
Why?
*And what if Jesus Christ, welcomed completely in a pure heart . . .
could make us want to laugh also!*

I don't know why, Lord,
   but when I was praying this morning
I suddenly realized
   that I never imagined you
   laughing,
laughing a really resounding laugh,
   echoing in waves, one after another,
towards others who welcome it,
   enriched by the joy it offers.

I imagine you, calm and peaceful,
and occasionally smiling quietly,
   but above all serious,
   and sometimes weeping.
In fact, Lord, I'm glad to know
   that you knew how to cry!

But your evangelists thought it better not to tell us
that one day, in one circumstance or another,
    you laughed out loud.
And I'm sorry they didn't tell us.

I also see you, Lord, handsome, luminous,
    transfigured by prayer,
or your eyes shining with anger,
    chastising
    moral and religious hypocrites.
I see you disfigured,
    trembling with loneliness and fear,
    blood-stained under torture.
But laughing out loud . . . definitely not.

    Nevertheless, I'm sure that you used to laugh.
Even if there are good people who think,
perhaps,
that such ideas are inappropriate!
    You laughed as a child in Nazareth,
when you played in the square with your friends.
    As an adolescent, you laughed with your cousins
when you were with the caravan, returning from the
                                    Temple.
    You laughed with your disciples
    at the wedding in Cana of Galilee,
and you sang,
and you danced when others danced.
    But afterwards . . .
    I find it hard to imagine!

    I've tried to discover why.
    I think I've found the reason . . .
    It's because I haven't enough faith!

I don't have too much trouble
believing that you are God.
Your Father whispered it to me,
I'm sure,
    because you told us that alone

one couldn't believe it,
and I thank you for this wonderful gift
   which transforms my life.
   But I admit
   that I don't find it easy
to believe that you are a man,
not a superman—a man,
a real man,
and that you didn't simply play at being a man,
   disguised as a man,
   pretending to be with us,
   in solidarity with us.

   Nevertheless, Lord,
though I may find it hard to believe sometimes
when I meditate on this mystery just with my head,
it is the most wonderful news for me,
news that fills me with gratitude and joy,
   when I contemplate it in my heart.
   Because in my eyes,
   it is the surest
   and most overwhelming proof
   that you love us beyond all else,
   and that this love is close to us,
   so close that it touches us,
   that it takes root in us,
in this humanity created by you,
   but so far away,
   so far away from you,
if you hadn't come among us.

For you could have loved us from on high, Lord,
   and could have sent us an ambassador
   other than yourself,
   but you travelled personally.
You could have come beside us,
so that you, God, could lead us
   and we, human beings, would follow you.
   But you came among us,
   a man with us,

a man like us,
so much like us
that we became brothers and sisters:
brothers and sisters of the baby who cried,
    and drank his mother's milk;
brothers and sisters of the little boy who learned to read,
    to pray;
brothers and sisters of the man who preached so well . . .
    too well,
    so that he died under torture,
    offering his life for us.
    Brother.
    Our brother Jesus,
    who knew how to weep . . . to laugh . . .
    because he was a man.

I have some strange ideas, Lord,
but what do you expect?
Thinking of you, so close to us . . .
    so like us
    so that we may become like you . . .
makes me happy,
so happy;
I'm amazed that we're not happier,
and it hurts me to see us looking too serious
    when we speak about you;
and I don't see why we should seem sad
    when we come together to pray to you,
    and to offer with you to the Father,
    your suffering . . . and your tears,
    your joys . . . and your laughter,
    your life.
Perhaps the people around us would have more faith in
                                                    you
if we were more joyful
    and they could see our joy.

Pardon my childish tricks,
    but like a little one
    on an older brother's knee,

I want to say to you this evening, Lord,
  'Make me laugh!'
Yes Lord, that's my strange prayer . . .
make me laugh,
so that I, in my turn,
  can make my brothers and sisters laugh.
  They really need to!

We write to you about the Word of life, which has existed from the very beginning. We have heard it, and we have seen it with our eyes; yes, we have seen it, and our hands have touched it. When this life became visible, we saw it; so we speak of it and tell you about the eternal life which was with the Father and was made known to us. What we have seen and heard we announce to you also, so that you will join with us in the fellowship that we have with the Father and with his Son Jesus Christ. We write this in order that our joy may be complete (1 Jn. 1:1–4).

Sing to the Lord, all the world !
Worship the Lord with joy;
come before him with happy songs!
                    (Ps. 100:1–2)

20. Is it really for you, Lord?

It's not just for fun that we are committed to one or other move-ment or service in the Church or in the world. On the contrary, we get very weary sometimes of all the meetings and activities which eat up our time and even leave us open to reproach, especially from our loved ones. But we should clarify the authenticity of our action. Quite often, it includes a lot of self-seeking and pride . . .
We christians need to be even more careful with regard to the presence of Jesus Christ at the heart of our action, because it is with him that we are working.
We find it difficult to live this 'faith vision' and to share it as a team during our meetings. But without him, we can do nothing.

Is it really for you, Lord,
    that I went out this evening
    to take part in that meeting?

    It was dark,
    it was cold,
the house was pleasant and my wife attractive.
She let me go, without a word,
    with just a faint smile and a little kiss,
    but in the look she gave me
    —that look that I can read—
    a bleak weariness
in which I saw a persistent reproach:
you're going again!

She'll be asleep when I get home
and I'll avoid making noise so as not to wake her up.
    At the same time I'll be hoping,
    quietly,
that when I slip into bed
    she'll turn towards me
    and murmur, half asleep:
'Did your meeting go well?'
    Then I'll go to sleep, reassured a little,

because I believe
that I'm understood a little and pardoned a little.

But is it really for you, Lord,
that I went out this evening?

In the car, I'm driving fast,
    I'm late and my friends are waiting for me.
Already the city around me is sleeping silently,
    and I catch myself admiring myself a little,
    thinking that I'm staying up,
    bravely,
    in the service of my brothers and sisters.
    But I travel with my doubts,
    worried,
ill at ease with myself and with you, Lord.

Is it really for you that I went out this evening, Lord?
Isn't it just because I'm in the habit of going? . . .
    it's the usual day!
Isn't it to promote my movement
    or the activity we're involved in? . . .
    there are so few of us!
Isn't it just pride? . . .
    they couldn't manage without me . . . !
Isn't it to defend and put over
my own point of view? . . .
    I think it's the only correct one!
Isn't it to show how reliable I am? . . .
    I'm never missing!
Isn't it to give me a good conscience? . . .
    the leaders of the Church tell us
    that we must be committed!
Is it really for you?

Sometimes I'm afraid that I'm deluding myself
    about the value of what I'm doing,
    about my intentions,
    about my generosity,
    about my faith;

I'm afraid of rushing,
    acting
    using my energy,
    for myself,
    without you.

I travel with my doubts, Lord,
    and all the while,
    as you invite me to think of you
    they continue to dance their ironical fandangoes,
making me conscious of a deep need for recollection,
so that I may find you in the silence . . .
But it's towards the noise that I go,
    the clash of words,
    the excitement of action,
    . . . and I know that in a few moments,
    once again,
    I'll forget you,
you, the one I want to serve.

Forgive me, Lord,
because while I believe with all my strength
    that you need me,
    need us,
    to build a fraternal world,
I often forget that I can't do it without you.
I work alone,
    I struggle alone,
    I fight alone,
and I'm afraid that's what others do also,
because often we don't think
of inviting you to the meeting,
    and when we say you are there,
    because we are accustomed to saying it,
    we avoid searching for
    and asking for your opinion,
because it's easier to settle for our own
and more difficult to reflect on your Gospel
and pray to your Holy Spirit.
But are we not building in vain, Lord,

unless we build
with you!

You are there Lord, and I'm speaking to you.
I entrust this meeting to you
    and, in a few minutes from now,
I'll have the courage to speak about you.
What I say will be *true*, and I will be *true*,
    because we will have dialogued
    and we will have nourished our love,
and when we return,
    together,
    in the car,
we'll talk again about the meeting,
about those who took part in it,
    and about *our* work.

And if my wife wakes up, when I come in,
    Lord,
    you'll give her a kiss,
    won't you,
    when I give her mine.

*I am telling you the truth: whoever believes in me will do what I
do—yes, he will do even greater things, because I am going to the
Father. And I will do whatever you ask for in my name, so that
the Father's glory will be shown through the Son. If you ask me for
anything in my name, I will do it (Jn. 14:12–14).*

*Remain united to me, and I will remain united to you. A branch
cannot bear fruit by itself; it can do so only if it remains in the
vine. In the same way you cannot bear fruit unless you remain
in me.*
*I am the vine, and you are the branches. Whoever remains in
me, and I in him, will bear much fruit; for you can do nothing
without me (Jn. 15:4–5).*

21. I'm growing old, Lord!

Old age can be a severe trial. Even though life is often difficult, many of us try to hold onto it when it begins to slip away. The worst suffering is to feel that one is useless, and putting other people to trouble when one would still like to be of service.

It is the time for humility and for faith that has been purified through lived experience.

Old age is not the road to death, but the path to life. Fullness of life at last, and 'divinised' in Christ forever. But the difficult transformation must be accepted, the passage to that other life, as the grain of wheat must die in the ground before it produces the ear of corn.

For the old person, the time is past for running towards others, but not for living in Christ as he lives in us. This is the condition, if the fruit is to mature.

I'm growing old, Lord,
    and growing old is hard!
I can't run any longer,
    I can't even walk fast.
I can no longer carry heavy weights,
    or go upstairs quickly.
My hands have started to tremble,
    and my eyes tire very rapidly
      as they go through the pages of my book.
My memory is failing and obstinately hides
    dates and names
    that it knows quite well.

I'm growing old, and the links of affection,
    established over many a long year,
    become slack, one by one,
    and sometimes they break.
So many of the people I know,
so many of the people I love,
go away and disappear
    into the distance,

that my first glance at the daily newspaper
    becomes an anxious search through the death notices.

I find myself alone, Lord,
    a little more alone every day,
alone with my memories
    and with past sorrows
    which always remain
very much alive in my heart,
while many of the joys
seem to have taken flight.

Understand me, Lord!
You who burned up your existence
    in thirty-three intense years,
you don't know what it's like to be growing old slowly,
and to be there,
while life escapes implacably
    from this poor rusted body,
an old machine with grinding gears,
    a machine that doesn't work;
and above all, to be there,
waiting,
waiting for the time to pass,
time which passes so slowly on certain days
    that it seems to be mocking me, as it turns and drags,
    before me,
    around me,
refusing to yield to the approaching night,
and finally allowing me . . . to sleep.

How can one believe, Lord, that time today
    is the same as time long ago,
time that went so fast on certain days,
    certain months,
so fast that I couldn't catch it,
    and it got away from me
    before I was able to fill it with life?

Today I have time, Lord,
too much time,
time piling up beside me,
unused,
and I'm there, motionless,
and no use for anything.

I'm growing old, Lord,
and growing old is hard,
so hard that some of my friends
often ask for this life to be ended,
a life which seems to them
to be of no use from now on.

They're wrong my child, says the Lord,
and you're wrong too.
Perhaps you don't say what they are saying,
but sometimes you agree with them.
All your brothers and sisters
need you,
And I need you today,
as I needed you yesterday.
Because a beating heart, though it be worn out,
still gives life
to the body it inhabits,
and the love in this heart can gush forth,
often stronger and purer,
when the tired body finally leaves space for it.
Some very full lives,
you see,
can be empty of love,
while others,
seemingly very ordinary,
radiate love infinitely.

Look at my mother, Mary,
weeping,
motionless at the foot of my cross,
she was there,
standing upright, certainly,

but she too was powerless,
tragically powerless.

She did *nothing*,
   she was simply there,
completely recollected,
completely welcoming,
offering herself completely,
   and in this way, with me,
   she saved the world,
   giving back to it
   all the love that men and women had lost
   along the pathways of time.

Today, with her,
   standing by the crosses of the world,
   you must gather the enormous suffering of humanity,
   dead wood to be burned in the fire of love.
But welcome the efforts and the joys also,
because gathered flowers are lovely,
   but they are of no use
   unless they are given to somebody,
   and so many people think about living
   but forget to give.

Believe me,
   your life today
   can be richer than it was yesterday,
if you accept growing old,
   if you accept being a motionless sentinel watching for
                                        the evening;
and, if you suffer because you have nothing in your hands
   that you can give,
then offer your powerlessness,
and together, I tell you,
we will continue saving the world.

*Remain united to me, and I will remain united to you. A branch
cannot bear fruit by itself; it can do so only if it remains in the vine.
In the same way you cannot bear fruit unless you remain in me.*

I am the vine, and you are the branches. Whoever remains in me, and I in him, will bear much fruit; for you can do nothing without me (Jn. 14:12–14).

'Yes,' Jesus said to them, 'and I assure you that anyone who leaves home or wife or brothers or parents or children for the sake of the Kingdom of God will receive much more in this present age and eternal life in the age to come' (Lk. 18:29).

I may be able to speak the languages of men and even of angels, but if I have no love, my speech is no more than a noisy gong or a clanging bell. I may have the gift of inspired preaching; I may have all knowledge and understand all secrets; I may have all the faith needed to move mountains—but if I have no love, I am nothing. I may give away everything I have, and even give up my body to be burnt—but if I have no love, this does me no good (1 Cor. 13:1–3).

22. *The stone was broad and ancient, Lord*

*Is it any wonder that when they look at themselves with merely
human eyes, men and women are made dizzy by the discovery of
their own 'smallness' compared to the hundreds of millions of
human beings, past, present and future? Who are they? Of what
value are their lives, tiny drops of water in an immense ocean, a
few moments in the millions of years?*
*It is only when they look at themselves with the eyes of faith that
this anguish can be handled properly.*
*Just as each and every child in a large family receives the 'total'
love of their parents and a new baby is similarly loved without
taking anything away from the other children, in the same way
the love of our Father who is in heaven reaches all, personally
and . . . infinitely.*
*Because each one of us is a unique member in the great body of
humanity, we are indispensable, each in our place, and our life is
not a life which passes, leaving only a few traces; it is eternal life
in and through Jesus Christ.*

The stone was broad and ancient, Lord,
on a very old path leading to the village
      above.
I'm told that from the most ancient times
      this path was the passage way
for a crowd of invaders,
      travellers and pilgrims,
and that hundreds
and hundreds of thousands of people
      before me had trodden on that paving stone,
      but weren't able to wear it away.
I look at it,
      hollowed out like a quarter of the moon,
      polished like a pebble,
and as I contemplate the hard stone, enduring,
      impassive witness,
I become dizzy at the thought of my own smallness.

Who am I, Lord, I who pass so quickly
   compared to the stone which endures?
It has borne the weight of hundreds
and hundred of thousands of people,
for hundreds and hundreds of years,
   and I am only one step
   among millions of other steps,
   steps that have vanished
   while it watches, motionless,
hard stone, stone which endures to remind me of my
                                    smallness.

What traces have they left, Lord,
   all these travellers down through the ages,
   endless crowds of men and women
   who have lived before me?
All those millions together have scarcely managed
   to make any impression on that hard stone.
   All these passers-by have passed!

Where are they now, tiny ants,
   who passed by the village
   above,
   and one by one toppled over the edge of time
   at the end of their journey through life?
Where are they now, those millions who have disappeared?
   I don't see them any longer.
   I don't hear them any longer.
. . . but I see this hard stone which endures
   to remind me of my smallness.

So who am I , Lord,
   I who am so small and would like to be so big?
   I who count my days, my years,
   and am only an instant!
   What's the point of living
if my life is only one second in millions of years?
   What's the point of struggling
if my efforts and my sufferings
are only imperceptible sighs

107

amid the clamour of innumerable human beings?
    What's the point of laughing if the sound of my laughter
is extinguished almost before it is raised,
ephemeral spark in the terrifying night of time?

What's the weight of my life, Lord,
   and of each of my steps,
   my words, my gestures,
   my tears and my smiles,
I who wanted them to be big and important,
   and dreamed
   of an eternal dimension for them?

But above all, Lord
how am I to believe, I who am so small,
   that I am so big in your eyes?
How could you have desired me and waited for me,
   among the millions of men and women to come?
How can you notice me today,
   a tiny grain of sand on the beaches of the world,
   a drop of water in the enormous river
   that flows and disappears into the ocean?
How can you love me,
among all the others to be loved,
and how will you remember me
   when the tiny flame
   of my life is extinguished,
   and goes—as I want to believe—
   to join the millions of flames
which burn before you
   and will continue to burn until the end of time?
Oh tell me, Lord,
in front of this hard enduring stone,
   which troubles me and mocks me.
I need to hear you repeating that you love me,
   as you have said that you loved me . . .
   despite my smallness.

Yes, I love you my child, says the Lord,
and your life is precious to me,

because it is only one life,
and that life came from the heart of my Father, long ago.
    But Life, you see,
    is not like the footsteps of men and women,
    separated one by one,
it is a river flowing in each one of you,
    even though you be millions.
You have received it from others, and you must give it to
                                 others,

    and others receive it from you
    so that they can give it also.
That's what love is, my child: life given.
    If you keep it for yourself, you die,
    if you give it you live,
. . . and your footsteps, your words,
    your gestures and your smiles
will live in your brothers and sisters until the end of the
                                 world.

But listen again,
your life is so precious to me
that I offer you mine.
    If you welcome my life into yours,
    then your footsteps, your words,
    your gestures and your smiles, will vanquish death,
and passing through the gateway of time
    they will emerge in my eternity.
Go in peace, I tell you that I love you,
    and that my Father loves you, you personally,
as he loves millions of your brothers and sisters,
because genuine love is never diminished
    by being shared among all,
and your Father is God,
and his love is *infinite*.

    Thank you Lord, thank you for your love,
. . . and thank you, hard enduring stone.
    I would take you away if I could,
    and I would make you into an altar stone.

Jesus told them another parable:
'The Kingdom of heaven is like this. A man takes a mustard seed and sows it in his field. It is the smallest of all seeds, but when it grows up, it is the biggest of all plants. It becomes a tree, so that birds come and make their nests in its branches' (Mt. 13:31–32).

We have many parts in the one body, and all these parts have different functions. In the same way, though we are many, we are one body in union with Christ, and we are all joined to each other as different parts of one body.
*So we are to use our different gifts in accordance with the grace that God has given us . . . * (Rom. 12:4–6).

23. Prayer with the night workers

Large numbers of people get up in the evening to go to work. Most of them haven't chosen this kind of life, but have been forced into it by necessity.
There are also men and womens enclosed religious, who get up at night to pray in their chapels. They have chosen to keep watch before God for their brothers and sisters.
The vast majority of those in the first group don't think of offering their efforts to the Lord, but these efforts are received and carried by the people in the second group and presented by them to God. Thanks to them, God hears the dramatic song of human affliction that rises towards him, every night, from the earth.

It's late, Lord,
and I want to sleep,
   I need to sleep.
But this evening, I'm thinking of the night workers,
of the multitude of men and women who work
   while we sleep,
   manufacturing things
   that we need in order to live.

Going on my way, I've often passed
   the night shift buses,
   as they make their way through the towns
   and the remote country areas,
   gathering up the labour
   to meet the demands of the factory.
Implacable metronomes for ballets without intervals,
they mark time in the lives of an army of workers.

I've met people
   with exhausted bodies and nerves,
   who weren't able to keep up the rhythm.
   They drag along with them a broken life
   that nothing or nobody can repair.
I've known shattered marriages,
   in which husband and wife

communicate with each other
only through scribbled notes
left on the kitchen table.
I've played very quietly with children
condemned to silence during the day
. . . because Daddy is asleep.

I don't understand, Lord.
When you invented the night,
wasn't it for sleep?
When your sun wisely goes to sleep,
switching off its light, it invites repose!
But human beings had the idea of working by night
and sleeping by day.
They switch on the neon lights
and then close the blinds,
to make believe that night is day
and day is night.

They say that if we want to respond
to the demands of the modern world,
nature must be harnessed, at all costs.
They say that the economy takes priority,
that it commands and must be obeyed,
and that the machine must be served,
day and night.
And they say that here or there
people are studying new working conditions,
trying to re-humanise
what has been de-humanised.

But you know why they're doing this, Lord . . .
so that the return will be better
and production increased!
Men and women are slaves still,
and the suffering goes on,
the immense suffering,
and cries,
and groans so quickly smothered,
and because we're used to it we stop thinking about it

and go to sleep;
　　it has been like that always . . .
　　because it has to be like that!

But this evening, Lord,
　　I *hear* this great clamour,
and before closing my eyelids,
　　abandoning myself to you,
I want to offer you,
　　not this unjust suffering
　　which you condemn,
　　but the amount of effort
　　it imposes on men and women,
　　and the wonderful generosity
　　it calls forth every day.
For why do these night workers get up,
　　if not to earn food for their spouses
　　and for their children.
And while there may be some
　　who are driven by the attraction of pleasures
　　that the rich so easily declare superfluous,
　　there are others for whom
it is a stupendous song of love,
raised up every night
　　. . . while we are asleep.

But does it reach you, Lord?
　　There are so many, alas,
　　who don't know for whom their lives sing,
　　beyond,
　　over beyond,
　　their earthly loves!
Listen, Lord,
please listen,
so that so much effort,
　　so much pain and so much love experienced,
　　may not be lost.

Forgive me, Lord,
　　why should I doubt you,

why shouldn't I believe that these hymns of the night,
    perhaps,
    rise higher towards you,
    than the hymns we sing so easily
    in cosy groups,
since they are more than just pleasant words,
    they are words of life
    marked with the blood of effort.

Forgive me, Lord,
    why should I doubt you,
    why should I doubt them,
when, mingled with this nocturnal chorus,
    some very clear voices are lifted up,
    voices of the men and women
    who rise before dawn,
watchers in the night,
    giving themselves freely,
    singing your praises,
    enclosed in their religious houses,
soloists of pure love,
    ambassadors for those who are there beside the crowd
                           of night workers,

    with mouths closed
    and perhaps even with hearts closed.

I believe, Lord
I believe,
    . . . but tell me this evening
    that you hear them all.

Yes my child, says the Lord, I hear,
    because all men and women are my brothers and sisters,
    even if they are not aware of it,
    and every song of love that rises from the earth
    reaches me.
And I welcome all of them,
    even the false notes,
    to transmit them to the Father,
    in infinite praise.

There are different kinds of spiritual gifts, but the same Spirit gives them. There are different ways of serving, but the same Lord is served. There are different abilities to perform service, but the same God gives ability to everyone for their particular service. The Spirit's presence is shown in some way in each person for the good of all (1 Cor. 12: 4–7).

As Jesus sat near the temple treasury, he watched the people as they dropped in their money. Many rich men dropped in a lot of money; then a poor widow came along and dropped in two little copper coins, worth about a penny. He called his disciples together and said to them, 'I tell you that this poor widow put more in the offering box than all the others. For the others put in what they had to spare of their riches; but she, poor as she is, put in all she had—she gave all she had to live on' (Mk. 12:41–44).

Then Jesus made the disciples get into the boat and go on ahead to the other side of the lake, while he sent the people away. After sending the people away, he went up a hill by himself to pray. When evening came, Jesus was there alone (Mt. 14:22–23).

24. Lord, we invite you to our new house

Many people, especially married couples, dream of owning their own house, a home where they can settle, put down roots and bring up a family. But this hope often hides a lot of traps. The house one has wanted for such a long time can become an all-absorbing preoccupation: it must be paid for, it must be furnished. Sometimes it demands considerable time and energy from its inhabitants, and there is a risk that it will take them away from other necessary tasks. And it can even become a prison for those who shut themselves into it.

It is not a bad thing to be 'rich' in one way or another—obviously it is a question of reasonable comfort—but it is a responsibility. Having a house of one's own is justifiable if it allows one to bring up one's family better and to serve one's brothers and sisters better.

We've dreamed of a house, Lord,
   I've dreamed of a house,
   and the house is there,
   our house.

Sitting on top of the still freshly turned earth,
   it went up quickly.
It waits for me faithfully, every evening,
and the opened shutters like open arms
   beckon and call to me from afar.
   It's our home.
   It's my home.
Our house, Lord,
all new and beautiful.

Now, it must be paid for,
   we'll make sacrifices.
Now, it must be furnished,
   we'll concentrate on that.
Now, we must live in it,
   . . . and that's not so simple,
because there are snares hidden in the walls of our house,

Lord,
the enemy has put them there,
as happens in embassies,
and while we may have detected some of them,
cleverly camouflaged,
a few escaped the radar of our hearts
when we were thinking things over, this evening,
and others, alas, are so attractive
that we have allowed ourselves to be taken in by them
already.

Understand us, Lord,
you who suffered
through having no place to lay your head.
We have suffered also,
from an apartment that was too small,
where noise lived with us;
we suffered
from those dirty stairs
which we found hard to climb in the evening;
from grey walls in front of us,
behind us,
hiding the sky from us;
from those neighbours who were
. . . forgive us Lord . . .
so difficult to put up with.

Understand us,
we waited so long,
we dreamed so long
. . . and waited so long because we've dreamed so long,
that today we really want
to return home,
to relax,
to curl ourselves up in the warmth of the house
as in a mother's womb,
and from time to time to light the wood fire
that sings and dances as it laughs
at the sad faces of the radiators
which heat without a smile;

to look at the garden and the flowers
planted in open ground,
    in real earth, Lord,
    earth that escaped the concrete
    and the dark tarmacadam.
We really want to be at home,
just by ourselves,
    and not have to go out in the evening
to take part in some meeting or other;
    not to respond sometimes to the invitation
    of those who are waiting for us outside,
    in their home;
    and not to open our door,
    except to very close friends
    who will come to add flowers
    to the bouquet of our joy.

Even so, Lord,
    you know
that our dreams of a house were generous dreams very
                                         often.

We wanted a home where we could rest,
    but rest so as to serve others better.
We wanted an open house,
    where others,
    all others,
could come
    as if they were coming into their own homes;
a house where you ring the door bell,
    enter,
    sit down,
    relax,
    rest,
a house from which you go out lighter,
    because burdens have been shared
    and sometimes even laid down;
a house from which you go out
    richer,
because you have been served with the meal of friendship.

But this evening, Lord,
  we're worried,
because we've discovered traps
  in the house.
We need your help not to fall into them,
and we need your help to be able to see
those that we don't want to see.
  Stay with us, Lord,
  It's late
  and night is approaching,
dark and heavy in our weariness.
Stay with us and make yourself at home in our home.
With all our heart we invite you to come into our new
                                                    house.

Open wide your heart,
  and I will come to your home,
  as I went long ago to the home of Martha and Mary
  and their brother Lazarus.
  If you wish,
  I will share my Word with you
  and you will share bread with me,
and I will be at home in your home
  if others are at home there too.

I'll come,
oftener than you think . . .
  but I'll come incognito . . .
  . . . and sometimes on evenings when you are tired.
Will you recognize me
in the unwelcome visitor at your door?

Anyone who comes to me and listens to my words and obeys them—I will show you what he is like. He is like a man who, in building his house, dug deep and laid the foundation on rock. The river overflowed and hit that house but could not shake it, because it was well built. But anyone who hears my words and does not obey them is like a man who built his house without laying a foundation; when the flood hit that house it fell at once—and what a terrible crash that was! (Lk. 6:47–49)

Whoever accepts my commandments and obeys them is the one who loves me. My father will love whoever loves me; I too will love him and reveal myself to him (Jn. 14:21).

25. He asked for 'one lemonade for two'

The major drama in today's world is the under-development of one part of humanity compared with the development and the over-development of the other part.

The problem has been there for so long that we are accustomed to it, and it takes some appalling disaster to jolt us into an awareness of what is happening. Then, faced with the sheer size of the problem and the worsening of the situation we often feel helpless and our reaction is to say:'What can we do about it?'

The developed countries think only of their own further development. They shut themselves up with their own problems, apparently unwilling to understand that they can never solve these without solving the problems of humanity as a whole.

A peaceful world cannot be built on large-scale injustice. In this respect, the Church also too often turns in on itself. It drowns in its own internal problems, at the expense of its missionary task. It doesn't give an example of sharing. Despite constant appeals from the Popes, those dioceses which are relatively well endowed with priests have sent only a few to the poor dioceses of Africa, Latin America and Asia. It organizes charity, it gives heroic service to the 'victims' of under-development and even helps them . . . to die. But it doesn't attack the causes of this under-development, saying that this is not its role. When some priests get involved, they are often called to order and even condemned.

The Church is quick to remind us of our moral responsibilities, for example in the area of sexuality. Notwithstanding some courageous official texts (little known because of the lack of media attention) it is generally less outspoken and vehement with regard to our economic and political responsibility.

The drama of the under-development of peoples, with its frightful consequences in terms of suffering and death, is the most serious collective sin of our time. For the christian, it is Jesus Christ who is dying every day in his millions of brothers and sisters.

Together, we are all responsible.

He asked for:
'One lemonade for two, please,'
    and the waiter in the cafe replied:
'That's not possible, Sir.'
    They looked at each other, he and she,
    he hesitated,
then, resigned, he ordered two lemonades.

They were thirty or thirty-five years old, perhaps.
They were poor, but certainly not tramps.
    I watched them, Lord,
    for a few long moments.
    They didn't exchange a single word,
    and barely a few looks.
I left, bringing them with me in my heart.

This evening, I present them to you,
    my unknown friends,
    my brother and sister.
I know that you saw them
    when I saw them,
    but a brother has the right,
    doesn't he,
to talk to his father about all his brothers and sisters in
                                                    distress?

I know nothing about these two, Lord,
nothing,
    except what I saw of their hidden suffering.
But I am aware, now, of the wound
    that they have reopened
    in my fragile heart,
    without realising
    that they were unleashing a storm.
Because my heart is a volcano,
ready to shoot up in flames
and savagely spew out
    a thousand flowing fires,
    locked up for too long.

You know, Lord,
that it makes me suffer,
and I often wish that you would give me
    a calm heart,
    a heart that beats quietly . . .
    and allows me to sleep.
    But that's how I'm made,
and I'm grateful to you.
Too bad about the suffering!

But I don't want this fire,
    which gushes from me so often,
to be transformed into petrified lava
    in a desert of the dead.
This evening, Lord,
welcome my anger also,
    and my distress
    and my outburst;
    from my prayer,
    my words,
    in flaming arrows,
I have only my revulsion to offer you;
you can transform this uncontrolled passion
    into a mysterious energy
    that is capable of lifting up mountains.

One lemonade for two,
those were their words.
But other words,
    so often read,
    so often heard,
    so often buried,
    forgotten,
were awoken in me,
and like wild beasts that have escaped from their cages
    they dance their infernal fandangoes
    in my head,
    this evening . . .
One litre of polluted water for one or for ten families.
One sack of corn or rice for an entire village.

One school for a whole region.
One hospital for a whole territory.
One university for a whole nation.
. . . One priest for one hundred thousand people.

One,
one,
always one,
for ten,
for a hundred,
for a thousand and ten thousand,
while others have ten,
a hundred,
a thousand . . . for one.
Because numerous groups of learned people
calculate,
they know how to put two and two together,
and they do it precisely
with their precise machines.
Men and women on all sides sit down,
reflect,
discuss,
and write precise reports based on precise figures.
And millions of people read them,
and say: it all adds up.
And the addition,
the figures,
these are men and women,
hundreds of millions of men and women
who are dying and shouldn't be dying!

These are hundreds of millions of children,
bellies swollen,
skin and bones,
surviving for two or three months
or for two or three years . . .
while some tiny babies,
in their perfect incubators,
will be able to live out their full span of life,

thanks to an army
of devoted doctors and nurses.

These are hundreds of millions of illiterates,
    who will remain at home
while others in their thousands
    dawdle and jostle each other
    in the universities.

These are hundreds of millions of disabled
    and sick people at the point of death,
while a sympathetic crowd
    goes into action with great generosity
    on behalf of a single heart
    that is failing
    or one small child
    whose eyes are dimmed.

These are hundreds of millions of men and women
    who would like to know you better,
    Lord,
you who said:
    I have come that they might have *life*
    and might have it in abundance.
I'll never believe
    that these words of yours
    refer only to the life of their souls.
As if your *life* could flourish
    on a heap of corpses!
As if you hadn't said to your Apostles:
    give them something to eat,
and to the crowd:
    share the bread and the fish,
and to all of us:
    'I was hungry . . .
    but you would not feed me.'

. . . Hundreds of millions of people
    who would like to know you,
while there are bishops

who are hesitant about sending them
one or two of their priests
because they no longer have
the two or three hundred
they consider necessary in the diocese;
while pious parishioners draw up petitions
   because they want to keep *their* devoted parish priest
   for themselves alone;
while a group of good christians protest
   because they no longer have
   their chaplain
   present at every meeting.

And while all this is going on, Lord . . .
while millions of people,
   who shouldn't die,
   are dying every day,
   steadily,
   inexorably,
our politicians
are concerned about *our* problems
because this is what we expect of them—
   about our real problems,
   but also about our small,
   very small problems,
and in their wise discourses
   they give just a few words
to the major,
scandalous,
intolerable drama
of a part of humanity
   dying before our eyes.

And while this is going on, Lord . . .
your Church laments
   and makes a thousand efforts
to hold onto a few thousands of its children
   who are leaving
   because they reject a Council
   and have doubts about its Eucharist

when the vestments are changed.
Your Church reminds its faithful
   that it is a sin to take the pill,
   and a very serious sin
   to do away with the unborn child,
but doesn't tell us loudly enough
that it is also scandalous
   to oblige millions of young boys
   and young girls,
   to prostitute themselves
   for a mouthful of bread,
and to allow the lives
of hundreds of millions of children to be aborted,
   children who are born,
   and who live
   and die before our eyes.

And while this is happening, Lord . . .
   I who shout so loudly,
   I'm satisfied with my blessed anger
   and I'm proud of it . . . !
I turn fine ideas around in my head . . .
   while I'm sitting down.
I reassure myself with a few clever excuses.
   I know, however,
I know that the calculations are precise
and that the figures are human beings.

Lord,
let me never be so lacking in decency
that I complain about my situation,
   even if I'm poor
   in comparison with those richer than I am:
let me never waste—
   disgrace of the 'haves' of this world—
and let me teach my children to waste nothing,
   by showing them the value of the bread
   and of the butter on the bread.
Let me do my best
to give practical help

to organisations that are fighting
    for the development of the third world,
    and of the fourth world,
instead of criticising them,
    judging them,
    from the heights of my complacency.
And because I'm convinced
that when there is more wide-spread understanding of the
                                                  drama
of this part of humanity that is dying,
    men and women will be forced, one day,
    to come together to find solutions,
let me never remain silent,
    but let me speak without ceasing,
    let me shout,
    even if I disturb people,
    even if some of them want to smother my cries,
    even if some of them want to dress me in red,
    and even if my friends don't understand me.

Now, Lord,
don't be angry with me;
    I did warn you.
You will separate the wheat from the tares in my prayer,
    you will do the sorting out.

    The volcano is extinct,
    but I implore you,
    even if I have to suffer,
    don't put out the fire!

*There was once a rich man who dressed in the most expensive
clothes and lived in great luxury every day. There was also a poor
man named Lazarus, covered with sores, who used to be brought
to the rich man's door, hoping to eat the bits of food that fell from
the rich man's table. Even the dogs would come to lick his sores
(Lk. 16:19–21).*

*My brothers, what good is it for someone to say that he has faith
if his actions do not prove it? Can that faith save him? Suppose*

there are brothers and sisters who need clothes and don't have enough to eat. What good is there in your saying to them, 'God bless you! Keep warm and eat well!'—if you don't give them the necessities of life? So it is with faith: if it is alone and includes no actions, then it is dead (Jas.2: 14–17).

As he saw the crowds, his heart was filled with pity for them, because they were worried and helpless, like sheep without a shepherd. So he said to his disciples, 'The harvest is large, but there are few workers to gather it in. Pray to the owner of the harvest that he will send out workers to gather in his harvest' (Mt. 9:36–38).

26. I'm not afraid of you any longer, Lord!

The religion of fear is finished. Almost finished. It's true that some people have moved away from the practice of their religion as their fear of breaking the rules has diminished. Is this a bad thing? While fear may be 'the beginning of wisdom' it is never the beginning of love, and religious gestures without authentic faith are an even worse form of hypocrisy than loving gestures without love. Didn't the Lord himself make this sufficiently clear!
Sin and confession are no longer fashionable. But if the 'sense of sin' has been lost, this is not the result of speaking less about sin but rather because sin was spoken of for far too long as a failure to keep the rules, the commandments. As for confession, we had emptied it of meaning. Many priests could no longer tolerate it and many of the faithful could no longer take it seriously and simply stopped going.
Following the Council, there was renewed hope. Many people were discovering or re-discovering the wonderful meaning of Recon-ciliation. They were coming back. But the warnings and the rules came back also! . . .
For pity's sake, let's not have churchmen ever brandishing threats of hell fire again in order to bring about 'a return to the faith'(!) It is weakness to get what one wants from others through fear, even if what one wants is for their good. It is lack of faith to believe that love is measured according to the merits of the loved one.
God's love is infinite and gratuitous. It is difficult to preach it but it is the core of the faith. And it is much easier to help people to follow a carefully enunciated rule than to show them how to live their lives as a loving response to our Saviour Jesus Christ. Prohibitions which reverberate louder than love songs will eventually kill love.

I'm not afraid of you any longer, Lord!
   I feel light,
   free,
   happy,
and I thank you for this.

Because I admit that I used to be a little afraid of you . . .
just a little, isn't that so?
    But it was too much.
For in my silent heart,
vaguely uneasy, I used to think sometimes
    that to follow you in fear and trembling
    wasn't really following you at all.

It's not my fault, Lord,
I was told so many things! . . .
and so many things that we're not told any more,
    but which are still there in our memories,
    poisoning our hearts.

I was told that it was wrong
    to do this
    because it was a sin,
    and even worse to do that
    because it was a serious sin,
and I would be punished for sin,
    a short time for small ones,
    forever for big ones . . .
unless I asked for forgiveness
in order to avoid paying the penalty.
    All I had to do . . .
    was to go to confession,
    and to go every time
    that I committed a serious sin.

And thus, Lord,
    when I was a young child
    I thought . . .
forgive me . . .
that to avoid eternal punishment
one didn't have to worry as one went through life,
but only to 'repent' properly at the last moment.

Certainly, we were reminded at that time
that we knew not the day nor the hour,
    as you yourself had told us.

131

And there were some sincere and zealous preachers
who brandished the threat of hell
    to make misguided sinners
    turn back again towards you.
The greater the fear,
the more numerous the returns
and the greater the joy!

    That was long ago . . .
    but it was a 'long ago'
which has left its mark on today's grandmothers and
                                grandfathers.
And I'm talking to you about it this evening, Lord,
    because some of the faithful
    regret that past.
They complain that the priests today only speak . . .
    about love,
    and not about sin
    or about eternal punishment.
If they were more severe, they say,
they would fill up the churches again,
and people would behave better
    if they were more afraid!

It's awful, Lord!
I don't judge what goes on in people's hearts,
and I believe in people's sincerity,
but how can they deform your message to such a point!
    Because all of that was true . . . !
    But is it really truthful
    to speak to a living person
    of nothing except sickness to be cured
    and death to be avoided?
Is it really truthful, Lord,
to fossilize love into calculated gestures,
    and to keep account of these gestures,
    faithfully and in minute detail,
and to measure their purity
in relation to all the established norms?

How can one believe, Lord,
    if one understands love at all,
    that it could ever be born of fear ?
    And if heaven is to love as you love,
    how can one believe
    that any kind of fear
    could one day prepare us for it?

How can one believe, Lord,
    that following you means respecting laws
    and performing certáin religious duties
    regularly,
    without paying attention
    to the life of one's heart,
    a heart that sometimes beats
    regularly
    on the bye-ways of life
and doesn't beat at all
on straight and beautiful highways?

How can one believe that heaven is earned,
    that we have to win it
    by paying the price,
    as if love was for sale
    and wasn't freely given!

. . . But how hard it is, Lord,
to have sufficient faith in that love,
and to live each day
in such a way
that we can receive this love from you!

Lord, I must ask for your forgiveness,
because although I haven't trembled in fear before you,
    like many people
    when thinking about death
    and about what happens after death,
I have made an effort sometimes
to behave correctly
    in order to protect myself.

There were times, Lord,
when I caught a glimpse of you near by,
    and I was attracted to you.
But I didn't follow you
even though you beckoned to me.
I was satisfied with a decent life
    and more or less regular practice of my religion,
and I thought that keeping the rules was all that was
                                                    required
    in order to be at peace.

But your love is faithful, Lord,
    and you are with us,
    and on my daily journey,
    little by little, I have recognized you
    and discovered you.

    YOU.

You who came to reveal that God is LOVE
    and only love,
you who taught us to call him
    our Father
    because we are his children,
you who gave us only one commandment:
    to love,
you who, when you were entrusting your Church
    to your first representative on earth,
    asked him only one question:
    'Do you love me, Peter?'

I was called to follow YOU, Lord,
and to follow you because of love.

I have no complaints, Lord,
on the contrary I'm very grateful
    to the priests who finally made me understand
    that you loved us first;
that the core of our faith is to believe this first of all
    and then allow ourselves to be loved;

that the most important part of our religion
is to love all our brothers and sisters
    as you have loved us.

I'm not afraid of you any longer, Lord!
and it's not because of fear
    that I'm trying to follow you.
Certainly, I'm not pure,
    very far from it,
    as you know!
But it seems to me that when I pray
    it's no longer just to maintain
    an important relationship
from which there are a number of advantages to be gained,
    but . . . I have the courage to say . . .
    because I love you,
because I want to develop our friendship
and, together with you,
to serve all my brothers and sisters better.

And now,
sometimes I dream . . .
    and I'm delighted with this dream,
    over the moon with joy;
I dream of seeing you face to face,
    of allowing myself to be loved at last,
    of loving you whole-heartedly,
and of seeing all men and women
gathered together one day as brothers and sisters,
    as a family,
    around our Father.

My only remaining fear
    —and I suffer because of it—
is the fear
    of failing to love enough,
    with a love like yours
    which has been freely given.

The Lord is my light and my salvation;
I will fear no one (Ps. 27:1).

Freedom is what we have—Christ has set us free ! Stand, then,
as free people, and do not allow yourselves to become slaves
again . . . For when we are in union with Christ Jesus, neither
circumcision nor the lack of it makes any difference at all; what
matters is faith that works through love. You were doing so well!
Who made you stop obeying the truth? How did he persuade
you? It was not done by God, who calls you . . .
But I still feel confident that you will not take a different view
and that the man who is upsetting you, whoever he is, will be
punished by God . . .
. . . you were called to be free. But do not let this freedom
become an excuse for letting your physical desires control you.
Instead, let love make you serve one another (Gal. 5:1–13).

Peace is what I leave with you; it is my own peace that I give you.
I do not give it as the world does. Do not be worried and upset;
do not be afraid (Jn. 14:27).

27. Lord, I would like to be sure that you are with me in the fight!

Many christians are committed to active involvement in the Church; they are needed, more and more. Others are committed to works of charity; they are needed also—those who have been hurt need good Samaritans. But far fewer are committed to work in trade unions or in politics. People distrust them and some even condemn them . . . if they don't share their opinions.

Dom Helder Camara says with a smile: 'When I'm concerned about the poor, they say I'm a saint. When I denounce the structures that make people poor, they say I'm a communist.'

It is praiseworthy to comfort the victims, but even more praiseworthy to fight against the 'sinful structures' spoken of by John Paul II. These structures produce the victims and they threaten peace. Fighting against them is the social dimension of charity.

The worlds of economics, the social order and politics are certainly tough and the struggle that takes place in them is sometimes violent. Christians are frightened by this. But not all violence is to be condemned. Parents who fight to defend a child from danger are 'violent', but their violence comes from love. And the Church has never condemned 'defensive' war (!) and doesn't condemn peoples who rise up against oppression. Hatred does not come from God.

Let christians not be shirkers, leaving their brothers and sisters to dirty their hands in struggles which are both just and necessary. Let them bring love to a struggle in which the Lord is with them.

Lord,
I fight, together with my comrades,
    loyal to my movement,
    to my organisation,
united in the struggle
for a life that is more just and more human.
But the battle is hard,
    and very often I'm afraid
    of being in it without you.

Lord,
I'd like to be sure that you're with me in the fight!
Alas, people are needed to stand up for the cause
　　when the war is raging.
Perhaps all of them will retire, one day,
　　refusing to become involved,
　　but that won't happen tomorrow.
　　And today,
　　there are many causes to defend,
　　and there are wars
　　to mobilize the combatants.
People are needed to care for the wounded
and to bury the dead,
　　because the victims are legion
　　and they call on us to look after them.
People are needed to sign the treaties
　　when some battles are over.
But many more people
are needed
　　to avoid wars by building peace,
　　the peace that flourishes
　　when justice reigns.

I hesitated for a long time
before becoming involved in this peaceful struggle.
Along with some of the other shirkers, I calmed my
　　　　　　　　　　　　　　　conscience,
　　learnedly holding forth
　　that one person alone
　　can't lift up the world.
I kept away from suspect groups . . .
　　of the revolutionary type.
I thought that the worlds of economics,
　　trade unions,
　　politics,
　　were polluted worlds,
and I was afraid that plunging into them would mean
　　　　　　　　　　　　　　dirtying my hands.
But I wasn't at peace, Lord.
And weren't you there,

challenging me constantly
through what was going on around me?
For you have told me that I must love my brothers and
sisters.

But loving them
is not only offering them a smile,
or holding out a hand.
If they have nothing to eat,
if they are ignorant and exploited,
and above all if they are deprived
of bread, of dignity,
can I send them back home
with my hand closed tight on my hundred cents,
saying to them:
'I love you'
or even:
'I'm praying for you!'

I became involved, but you know it's hard,
because while those who fight
and serve
amid the ravages of war
are admired and decorated,
those who fight to change this unjust and cruel world
into a world of peace and harmony
are often criticized
and sometimes judged severely.

You pushed me into it, Lord,
so I ask you not to leave me alone,
because when I become very involved
I find myself in the thick of the fight,
attacked . . .
with blows raining down
from adversaries
and sometimes from friends,
misjudged . . .
I'm considered too right wing,
too left wing,
too much to the centre,

and everyone paints me in a different colour.
I search, and I search for myself,
and I have doubts occasionally.

Because the fight is not straightforward,
and I suffer as a result.
And the battles are so tough
   that I often lose sight of you,
   . . . and I admit it.
   Alone,
   in the evening,
   before you,
   I regret this,
   I'm ashamed of it
   and I ask for your forgiveness.
Because if I want to fight,
I want you to be with me.

Hear my prayer, Lord,
   for I know
   that our human constructions
   are not the Kingdom.
I know also that the yeast
needs the dough to make it rise.
   And the dough needs flour,
   and the flour needs wheat,
   and the wheat, the flour and the dough
require the work of our hands
   so that the bread may be baked,
   and justly shared out,
   and so that from this bread that is offered
   you may make your Eucharist.

   Lord,
give me I pray,
the yeast of your love!

Help me not to judge and condemn
the people who sit calmly on the side-lines . . .
   discussing,

watching us as we battle in the arena.
And take away the jealousy I feel
    when I see them
    profiting without a qualm from our victories,
    forgetting that they owe them to us.

Help me to understand,
to accept,
    that people of the same faith
    profess ideas
    that are opposed to mine;
let me be able to receive communion at the same table
    with those who are on the other side in the fight.

Let loyalty to my movement,
    to my party,
    never be an absolute for me;
for me whose involvement in the fight is a matter of
conscience,
    who while accepting its instructions
    and obeying faithfully,
frequently rebels
when your Church speaks,
    and sometimes refuses to follow its directives.
Give me the strength,
    the strength to say no
when my conscience refuses to say yes,
    and the courage to accept
    the reproaches of friends
    who accuse me of treason,
    even though for me it is a matter
    of true loyalty.

Help me to know your Gospel,
not to look for prescriptions
that can't be found in it,
    but to be nourished by your Word,
so that this good seed
may sprout from my well-prepared ground,
may bloom as good news for my brothers and sisters

and may ripen for them
as fruits of justice and peace.

Finally, Lord, grant me
    that supreme grace . . .
    the grace that only you can give,
    to love my adversaries
    as well as my allies,
not only in the secret temple
of my better feelings,
    but by listening to them,
    respecting them,
    trying to understand them;
    and the grace to believe
    that sincerity
    and generosity
    are not reserved to me,
but can be found in others,
    even if they are enemies.
For you know how I get carried away, Lord,
and how I tend, too quickly perhaps,
to refer to this as my passion for justice!
    Sometimes, I am so anxious to get my own back,
    and to hurt
    those who have hurt me . . .
    that I find it hard,
    yes, very hard to forgive.

    Lord, give me the strength to forgive.

I am with you, says the Lord,
I am with you in your struggles,
because I am with all those who fight
    to defend their brothers and sisters,
    even when they venture onto battle grounds
    far from the protected enclosure
    where the fearful lie dormant.
But look at what is going on in your heart, my child,
    because I cannot be present
    where there is hatred,

and only love can ensure your victory
   while at the same time ensuring mine.

Why do you doubt, you of little faith?
   Happy are you!
   Happy are all of you
   who have the courage to risk
   getting your hands and your feet dirty
   in the struggle for justice;
because I didn't come
for those who stayed clean
   by remaining seated
   with their hands in their pockets.

Don't be afraid of anything!
I washed the feet of my disciples,
and if the feet of the combatants
are covered in dust,
   I'll wash them also.

*My brothers, what good is it for someone to say that he has faith
if his actions do not prove it? Can that faith save him? Suppose
there are brothers and sisters who need clothes and don't have
enough to eat. What good is there in your saying to them, 'God
bless you! keep warm and eat well!'—if you don't give them the
necessities of life? So it is with faith: if it is alone and includes no
actions, then it is dead (Jas. 2:14–17).*

*This is how we know what love is: Christ gave his life for us. We
too, then, ought to give our lives for our brothers! If a rich person
sees his brother in need, yet closes his heart against his brother,
how can he claim that he loves God? My children, our love should
not be just words and talk; it must be true love, which shows
itself in action (1 Jn. 3:16–18).*

28. 'It's not all me!'

We can be driven to the point of despair when we see people dear to us destroying their own lives and tragically damaging the lives of those who love them. It is then when we feel almost completely helpless and when we have given in to tears that we must implore God to help us to believe in the prodigal son despite his fall from favour.

For Jesus Christ, there is no such thing as someone who is lost. Regardless of how they behave, he believes in everyone, because he sees them with eyes that are not the same as ours. When he looks at them, his look reaches to the very centre of their being. He believes in them because he knows that in suffering for them and with them, he has saved them all.

Certainly, we must not neglect the human means suggested to us by our own intelligence, but if we look at everyone—especially those of whom we despair—with the eyes of Christ, we will help them to recognize the life that is in them.

Here I am this evening, Lord, with you,
   in front of him,
   in front of her:
   my son,
   my wife,
   my grand-child,
   or my friend . . . what does it matter!
He is a poor, big, lost child,
like a boat adrift from its moorings
in the storm of life.
   He drifts,
   a drug addict,
   an alcoholic,
   dissolute and lying,
   sometimes violent,
   hateful . . .

   He is greedy,
   insatiable,
burning with a furious will to live,

and sometimes with a throbbing wish to die,
a wish to die because he can't come to terms with living.
　He searches.
　What is he searching for?
　Pleasure.
　What pleasure?
　Happiness.
　What happiness?
　He doesn't know.
　He no longer knows.
His body is shattered and his heart is torn to pieces.

Around him is the desert.
　One by one, his family and friends have lost heart.
　They weep for him.
The orthodox have condemned him:
　they are anxious to avoid contagion,
　or they want to put him in prison.
But I love him, Lord,
and I can't just let him die.
　He is my son,
　she is my daughter . . .
　my little girl,
　my little boy . . .
and even though he falls and falls again,
and in spite of my fear and desperation,
　in spite of everything,
　I go on believing in him, in her.

Several times,
looking at him and seeing beyond his degeneration,
　I said to him:
　'You're wonderful!'
　He was surprised,
there was a shadow of doubt in his eyes,
but also a flash of light
shining in them for an instant,
　and once—
giving me the tiniest bit of precious hope in the night,
while I was clumsily reproaching him for his life-style—

he murmured,
tearfully,
distressed:
It's not all me!

It's true, Lord,
  isn't it!
It's not he.
  I believe this.
  I want to believe it.
  But increase my faith,
  my faith in him,
my faith in you who challenge me,
test me, each day,
  through him.

Let me believe, Lord, that you are there
  whenever he is there
  in front of me,
  alive.
Let me believe that it is God,
  our Father,
who breathes life into him at that moment,
  as he breathed life into him yesterday,
and as he will offer it to him again tomorrow,
faithful companion of the prodigal.
Let me believe that like every man and woman
  he is created each day in your image,
beyond his horrible masks
and the mud of the journey.
Let me believe
that on the terrifying night of your passion,
  long ago, you saved him.

Let me believe
that today,
  in spite of everything,
  and in spite of him, perhaps,
at the bottom of his heart,
a heart that is buried in a sealed tomb,

the child of God stirs,
  grows,
  is ready to be born,
and that all that is required to bring this child to life
is a loving look to touch him,
a voice to reach him,
as yours reached long ago
to the heart of the sinner:
'I do not condemn you either' . . .
because I love you
and because I trust you.

Lord, let me be the one who says it to him,
  and let him believe it;
  let him believe it with all his strength,
  because you believe it.

Do not judge others, so that God will not judge you, for God will judge you in the same way as you judge others, and he will apply to you the same rules you apply to others (Mt. 7:1–2).

. . . love your enemies and pray for those who persecute you, so that you may become the sons of your Father in heaven. For he makes his sun to shine on bad and good people alike, and gives rain to those who do good and to those who do evil (Mt. 5:44–45).

Some Pharisees and some teachers of the Law who belonged to their group complained to Jesus' disciples. 'Why do you eat and drink with tax collectors and other outcasts?' they asked. Jesus answered them, 'People who are well do not need a doctor, but only those who are sick. I have not come to call respectable people to repent, but outcasts' (Lk. 5:30–31).

29. She said to him: 'I'll be with you, my child.'

Jesus is present in our lives. We are told this repeatedly. Do we really believe it or do we only half believe it? But whether we are at the beginning of our relationship with him or deeply committed to our life of friendship with him, we always suffer because we can't see or touch him.

We need to understand that physical presence is not the only way in which people are present to each other. Those who love each other authentically have experience of this.

It is love that makes people present to each other, and the intensity of their presence depends on the intensity of their mutual love.

God, who loves all of us infinitely, is totally present to each one of us.

Long ago, there were morning and evening prayers which began with the words: 'Let us place ourselves in the presence of God and adore him'. Our lives would be transformed if we developed the habit of placing ourselves in the presence of God, frequently during the course of the day.

The man was leaving, Lord, to go I don't know where,
to live I don't know what important moment of his life.
   Leaning towards his elderly mother,
   he kissed her tenderly,
   and she
   kissed him even more tenderly.
Then, holding his face between her trembling hands,
   she whispered:
   'Go my child, I'll be with you.'
There was a long silence . . .
then she added:
   'Do you believe that?'
   'Yes mother,' he said.
   He left.
And she,
with tears in her eyes,
accompanied him from a distance.

Some time later the man told me
that it was like this
whenever he went away,
and that he was always strengthened
in times of difficulty
by the belief that he was accompanied
by his mother's love.

   And as I meditate
   this evening,
      I suddenly realize, Lord,
that these are the words
      you used
      when you were leaving us
      to return to the Father:
'I will be with you . . . until the end of time.'
And I'm sure that you expect us to respond
as the son responded to his mother:
      Yes, we believe it.

You know that I'm weak, Lord,
      and often,
      in difficult moments,
I look for the support of a friendly presence.
      I feel the need of a word,
      of a hand to hold,
      of a face to kiss,
but now I understand
that physical presence
is not necessarily the sign of real presence.
      Two people can see each other,
      touch each other,
      and even embrace each other warmly,
      while at the same time remaining at a distance,
      far from each other,
      separated from each other,
      unless their love,
      deep down,
      unites them.
How many handshakes are just play acting!

149

How many couples,
who have slept in the same bed for ages,
are just two lonely people,
camping on one side or the other
of an impassable moat!

But I also believe, Lord,
with all my strength,
that two people
separated by time or space,
can be together,
can be united,
can live in deep communion,
if their love is alive.

I believe this of human beings, Lord,
so why shouldn't I believe it of you.
Since you love us *infinitely*,
your presence to each one of us
must be *infinite*.
Real Presence,
total presence,
always and everywhere.

Nothing can separate us from you, Lord,
nothing that comes from you,
but only what comes from us,
and above all . . .
our lack of faith.

This evening, Lord,
you are saying to me once again:
'I will be with you until the end of time'
and you are asking me quietly
'Do you believe that?'
Yes Lord, I do believe it,
but please increase my faith.
Let me always live
in your loving presence,
you who accompany me in my daily comings and goings,

as the elderly mother
accompanies her son with her faithful love.
Help me to work in your presence,
to rejoice in your presence,
to rest in your presence,
because if I thought you were there, Lord,
if I was open to the love you offer,
I would never be alone again,
I would never be weak again,
and in front of you I would never be able
to do the bad things I'm tempted to do,
not like the little boy
who is afraid that his mother
will see what he is doing and punish him for it
but like the grown-up son
who discovers his mother's great love for him
and then only wants to thank her for it
through his life.

. . . your presence fills me with joy and brings me pleasure for
ever (Ps. 16:11).

Who, then, can separate us from the love of Christ? Can trouble
do it, or hardship or persecution or hunger or poverty or danger
or death ?
No, in all these things we have complete victory through him
who loved us! For I am certain that nothing can separate us from
his love: neither death nor life, neither angels nor other heavenly
rulers or powers, neither the present nor the future, neither the
world above nor the world below—there is nothing in all creation
that will ever be able to separate us from the love of God which is
ours through Christ Jesus our Lord (Rom. 8:35, 37–39).

Lord, I have given up my pride
and turned away from my arrogance.
I am not concerned with great matters
or with subjects too difficult for me.
Instead, I am content and at peace.
As a child lies quietly in its mother's arms,
so my heart is quiet within me. . . (Ps. 131)

And so I walk in the presence of the Lord, in the world of the
living. (Ps. 116:9)

30. Lord, I haven't yet made joy my own

Pleasure is relatively easy to obtain. It comes in many different forms and is connected mainly with the body. Like food, most pleasures are rapidly consumed and frequently leave one vaguely dissatisfied.

Joy is connected with the soul. It is not easily possessed. It is a virtue to be acquired, an incomprehensible mystery for those who haven't experienced it, and it can coexist with the greatest suffering in the same heart.

Only God is perfect happiness. Perfect joy. Only the pure of heart—in spite of their human limitations, in spite of the fact that during this life they can glimpse only a few reflections of the beauty and greatness of God, in spite of the pain of seeing their brothers and sisters suffering— can attain this joy, by being open to God and receiving it from him. But isn't this the preserve of the saints? . . . and as for us, can we say in all honesty 'we have really made joy our own'?

I'm told, Lord, that one should smile,
    smile every day,
    and then smile again.
I'm told that joy is a solid christian virtue,
    and that a sad saint
    is a very sad saint.
I'm told that people can't bear witness to you
    unless their faces and their lives
    radiate your *joy*.
I want to believe this . . .
but I haven't yet
    made joy my own, Lord.

All too often, joy is my faithless companion;
    it flies away,
    returns,
    and flies off again.
Just when I think I've grasped it,
    it disappears,
and a few clouds

trail across the blue sky of my heart,
   and sometimes
   they explode into storms . . .
   It rained on my joy.

Lord,
   it's your fault
that I haven't yet made joy my own!
You've told me that men and women are my brothers and
                                       sisters,
   and that I should love all of them,
   even my enemies.
I've tried, I keep on trying and sometimes I think I'm
                                succeeding.
   But then I've discovered, Lord,
   that to love
   means to be ready
   to share the suffering of those one loves
   . . . and often their suffering is colossal!

Lord,
I don't understand.
Is it possible to be completely happy
when into the recesses of peaceful days
   or into the silence of the night
comes the sound
   of cries that cannot be silenced:
   the murmuring of the unemployed,
   the moans of the starving,
the tears of separated spouses and dispersed children,
   the rattles of the dying,
   the shrieks of the tortured,
   the terrible din of battles . . .
atrocious concert of a thousand discords,
which rises up to us,
endlessly,
from humanity torn apart,
   members scattered,
   members bleeding,
of a body which you willed to be united and happy.

Lord,
I don't understand.
 Your apostle Paul said:
 'If one part of the body suffers,
  all the other parts suffer with it'
  and I suffer . . . a little,
and I know I would suffer more
if I loved more,
but I believe that I would stop suffering
if the cries of my brothers and sisters stopped.

 No, I couldn't be completely happy
when so many members of my family
 are unhappy.
But there are some who could, Lord.
As they watch television during a meal
and see the pictures of disasters
that are shown every day,
 they say: 'Isn't that terrible! . . .'
and then
after an awkward silence:
'What's for dessert today?'
When they open the newspaper
 and read the main headline
they exclaim: 'Another bombing attack, and more
                             innocent people killed.
 It's appalling!'
And then, a moment later:
'There's a very funny film on TV on Sunday,
 we ought to watch it!'
At their important meetings, they announce:
 'What ought to be done is . . .
 if it hasn't been done already . . .'
They discuss the problem for two hours . . .
and then before going home they have a drink together
 and laugh at each other's stories.
During the prayer of the faithful,
these good christians pray regularly
 for all who suffer from any kind of poverty . . .
 and then proclaim in song the joy of being together,
 with you,

the joy of being able to offer your sacrifice to the Father.
And they still say:
One must live well!
It's not a sin to be happy;
it's unhealthy to make oneself feel guilty,
and even more so to make others feel guilty;
I've contributed already!
you have to trust people!
Jesus has overcome death, he is risen!
    Let's sing, let's embrace each other, let's be happy!

They say . . .
they say . . .
    and I also say, Lord,
    and I also live,
    and I also laugh,
but there are days when I'm afraid
    that my joy may not be genuine,
    that it may be just a burst of laughter
    to block out the cries of men and women.
I'm afraid that my joy
    may spring thoughtlessly from a good conscience
    that is satisfied with a few gifts offered
    and a few good deeds done.
I'm afraid that my momentary joy may simply mean that
                                    I'm asleep,
    that it may be an escape into golden dreams
    supported by the illusion of a deep faith.

. . . Lord, I haven't yet made joy my own!

Lord,
if I haven't yet made joy my own,
    this is also because . . .
you made us too small
    for your joy, a joy that is too much for us.
How can we be completely happy
    when so many hungers
    torture our bodies and our minds,
    so many hungers that can only be appeased

but never satisfied?
How can we be completely happy
    when life mocks us
    with unattainable dreams dancing in front of us every
                                    morning,
    but never realized when evening comes?
How can we be completely happy
    when a hand held,
    when lips joined in a kiss,
    scarcely touch the inviolate mystery
    of the person who is with us?
How can we be completely happy
    when your face,
    occasionally glimpsed in prayer,
    is hidden afterwards
in the night that is too long.

. . . Lord, I haven't yet made joy my own!

Accept your limitations, my child,
says the Lord;
    you are not God,
    you are not almighty,
but you are a member of my body,
    and each one of these members
    receives a few morsels of joy,
    like a nourishing mouthful of bread,
like a refreshing draught of wine.
Welcome them.
It is I who give them to you.

But it's true, my child,
    that even though
    I am alive,
    risen from the dead,
    for you and for all,
    I am also crucified
    every day, in the members of my body.
My passion has not been accomplished
    while my brothers and sisters suffer,

156

and while you suffer with me.
I've warned you
    that this is the lot of disciples.

    Don't be ashamed to suffer,
    but do what you have to do
    for your brothers and sisters,
    where you are,
    generously.
Then you will know peace,
    great *peace*,
my peace,
that I promised:
    'Peace is what I leave with you,
    it is my own peace that I give you.'
As for the joy that you seek:
    to attain complete joy, my child,
you may have to wait for the day
when I will say to you:
'Well done, good and faithful servant . . .
enter into the joy of your master' (Mt. 25:21).

Then Jesus said to his disciples, 'And so I tell you not to worry about the food you need for your body. Life is much more important than food, and the body much more important than clothes. Instead, be concerned with his Kingdom, and he will provide you with these things. Do not be afraid, little flock, for your Father is pleased to give you the Kingdom' (Lk. 12:22–23, 31–32).

I love you just as the Father loves me; remain in my love. If you obey my commands, you will remain in my love, just as I have obeyed my Father's commands and remain in his love. I have told you this so that my joy may be in you and that your joy may be complete (Jn. 15:9–11).

31. *Those two are in love, Lord*

It is through their bodies, words and gestures that men and women express and convey friendship and love. A handshake and, above all, a kiss between lovers are wonderful 'signs' when they are authentic. Unfortunately, people don't always put the best of themselves into gestures which ought to be sacraments of human love and friendship. Then the gestures become countersigns and sometimes even betrayal.

God himself became incarnate, and has been revealed in human words. He used human words to convey his friendship and affection. But he put himself into his words and gestures completely: 'only say the word and I shall be healed.' He continues to give himself completely, in his Church, through words and gestures: the sacraments.

If our gestures of friendship and love were true and if Christ was really in us, we would be able to convey to our brothers and sisters something of the 'tenderness of God', who became flesh to be with us.

Those two are in love, Lord.
   I know.
   You know.
They kissed each other in front of me.
   I watched them.
   You watched them.
And we were happy, weren't we?
Because to kiss is beautiful
when it is a sacrament of love.
   Breath exchanged:
'I give you my life and I receive yours.'
   Lips joined:
'I offer you myself as food and you satisfy my hunger.'
   This is the way lovers speak,
     in communion with one another,
seeking to realize their dream of unity.

Yes it's beautiful, Lord,
because those two are in love.
    They signified this today,
    in your presence,
and I thanked you very quietly
    for our bodies
    which can whisper wordlessly,
    I love you,
    to all those we love.
Because you gave us bodies, Lord,
    and hands,
    and lips,
to speak for beating hearts
    that are unable to express themselves in words.
Without our bodies our souls would be silent
    and our love imprisoned,
and without our bodies nobody could know
    the love
    or the love songs of another person.

And you also, my God,
    oh unspeakable mystery,
    you who are so great,
    so distant,
    so unapproachable,
that no one has ever seen you,[1]
    heard you,
    touched you,
one day
    you took flesh
    for us,
and through your son,
    your word made *flesh*,
you made known to us your infinite love.
You, Jesus,
    who wanted, long ago,
    to be nourished
    through your eager lips on Mary's breast,
    by the milk of a mother

1. Jn. 1:18

159

who was one of us;
you who, later on,
    placed your hands on the sick
    and restored them to health
    by giving them your life;
you who allowed yourself to be touched by the crowd
    of poor and sick people,
    of honest people and thieves,
    of adulterers,
    of prostitutes . . .
you who caressed fishermen
    and embraced children;
you who through your crucified body
    crucified our sins;
you who offered this body to all
    as a sacramental sign,
    a loving kiss,
    to those who receive it,
    food for *life*,
    union in communion
    communion;
you who no longer have flesh
    and hands
    and lips
    to express your love today,
    but want to whisper it to all,
    through our flesh and hands and lips;
teach us, I implore you,
    to love with these selfish bodies,
    bodies created to express our affection
    and to make love,
but which, alas,
    are often too clumsy and too eager,
seeking to take more from others than they are prepared
                                 to give,
    and revealing more of our hungers than of our souls.

Forgive us for all those signs of friendship,
    affection or love,
which are just deceptive packages

with nothing inside,
or even lies
    and counter-signs
    for those who receive them
    and those who are watching us.
Forgive us for the mechanical handshakes
    distributed on all sides as we go through the day,
    without exchanging
    even a fleeting glance;
for the prostituted handshakes
    during election campaigns,
    looking for the attention of others
    and feigning interest in their affairs;
for the deceitful handshakes,
    when the heart rejects
    but the body pretends.
Forgive us above all
for the kisses taken from others by surprise,
for the stolen kisses
    seeking only for pleasure,
for kisses of betrayal
    hiding the breakdown of relationships,
and for the wantonness of kisses
    that are made commonplace,
    abused,
    wasted,
    empty of affection
    and empty of love.

Yes, Lord,
    teach us to love with these selfish bodies!

Tomorrow, Lord, unless you help me
    I'll be back again on the same path,
    confused,
    bewildered,
I who so often fail to use my body properly,
    faking its words,
    and falsifying
    its love songs.

So, this evening,
   once again,
with all my strength I implore you
   to wash my hands and purify these lips
   that have been prostituted so often;
open my heart to your infinite love
   and re-unite my body and my mind
   which have been separated so frequently.
Then, rich in myself and enriched by you
   I'll rejoin the others,
and through my loving gestures
I'll tell them a little about
your love made *flesh*.

You know that your bodies are parts of the body of Christ. Shall I take a part of Christ's body and make it part of the body of a prostitute? Impossible.
Don't you know that your body is the temple of the Holy Spirit, who lives in you and who was given to you by God? You do not belong to yourselves but to God; he bought you for a price. So use your bodies for God's glory (1 Cor. 6:15, 19–20).

The Word became a human being and, full of grace and truth, lived among us. We saw his glory, the glory which he received as the Father's only Son (1Jn. 14).

A Pharisee invited Jesus to have dinner with him, and Jesus went to his house and sat down to eat. In that town was a woman who lived a sinful life. She heard that Jesus was eating in the Pharisee's house, so she brought an alabaster jar full of perfume and stood behind Jesus, by his feet, crying and wetting his feet with her tears. Then she dried his feet with her hair, kissed them, and poured the perfume on them (Lk. 7:36–38).

32. He hugged me very tight and said: 'I adore you!'

The Lord has given us the commandment to love all our brothers and sisters, and many christians take this commandment seriously. Some of them, however, only relate to others at the level of their intelligence. That is to say, their efforts to help are dictated by their heads rather than by their hearts. They are not moved by any enthusiasm or any feeling of solidarity with the hungry. They are simply carrying out a duty. However, not only children but all human beings need friendship and affection. They miss it terribly when they don't have it!
We should reach out to others with our whole being—body, heart and mind—and not just with a small part of ourselves. Jesus allowed himself to be touched and embraced and he knew how to embrace. Through us he can continue to reach men and women with a 'heart of flesh'.

He's a little child, Lord,
   an abandoned child
taken into their warm home by a loving family.
His past suffering has marked him
   and his face
   is one long cry for love.

I tried to look at him
   as I believe
   you would have looked at him.
I smiled at him, I listened to him,
and within a few moments
contact was established.
   Suddenly,
   he threw himself into my open arms,
   he hugged me very tight and said:
   'I adore you!'
and with equal enthusiasm I said to him:
   'and I adore you'.

My mother used to tell me that we should adore no one
                                    except God,
    and I remembered her words at that moment,
    . . . I don't know why.
But as I pray this evening, Lord, I dare to think
    that the child through me
    and I through the child,
    together
we discovered and reached something of you.

For you suffer with him, Lord,
    through him,
    and his cry is your cry,
    and I believe
    that I heard it this morning.

Lord,
I want to be at the feet of the crucified child
as at the foot of the cross.
But I hope also that the child,
    finally taken down from the dead wood
    to which evil had nailed him,
    may in my loving arms
discover and touch a little of your love.

    I've wanted so much, Lord,
    to gather myself together,
    so as to reach out to others
    with my whole self,
refusing to love just with my head,
    refusing to respond without feeling to your
                            commandment of love,
but afraid of loving only with my sensitive heart
or with a body that is too eager.

Help me, Lord,
to gather together in myself
what has been dispersed,
to unite my forces
and to risk the adventure of reaching out to the starving,

not with a few charitable gestures,
wisely planned,
but with my heart of flesh,
so that they may live.

Help me to be truly open to your brotherly love,
so that through sharing in my life,
in your life,
they may be nourished.
Because, Lord,
you no longer have arms to welcome the children of the
earth,
especially people seen as outsiders,
like those who were pushed aside by the apostles
when they crossed your path long ago.
You no longer have knees for them to sit on,
and eyes to look at them,
words to speak to them
and to make them laugh,
or lips
to kiss them tenderly.
But the wonder is
that you need us,
you need me,
imperfect mirror that I am,
to reflect a few rays of your love.

This evening I thank you, Lord,
because this morning
I was able to give you a little of myself,
to reach the child
who was secretly trying to approach you
and to touch you.
But forgive me, Lord,
for having so often wasted
or kept for myself
what I should have given to others.
While it may be easy
to refuse nothing to the child,

it is hard for me to give, and to give myself
    to *all* my companions on the journey.

Nevertheless, Lord, I know that all men and women
    are children
    who continue growing until death,
and whether they are great or small,
    their faces scarred or unscarred,
    all are children of the good God
    who awaits their love.

Then he took a child and made him stand in front of them. He put his arms round him and said to them, 'Whoever welcomes in my name one of these children, welcomes me; and whoever welcomes me, welcomes not only me but also the one who sent me (Mk. 9:36–37).
God is my witness that I am telling the truth when I say that my deep feeling for you all comes from the heart of Christ Jesus himself (Phil. 1: 8).

33. Prayer for my unknown brothers and sisters

Whether we like it or not, all of us are brothers and sisters. But the human family is very numerous and there are all kinds of barriers which keep us apart and sometimes make enemies of us. On the purely human level, it is our duty to find our 'unknown' brothers and sisters, to establish links with them and to make a dispersed community into one family again. It is for this purpose that Jesus came among us. He asked us to love all our brothers and sisters as we love ourselves and as he has loved us. So that we might be able to do this, he gave his life for us. Those who receive him become children of God in him. Together, regardless of race, social background, or behaviour . . . they can address God as 'our Father'.
There are no longer 'strangers'.

Is it true, Lord,
that since the beginning of time,
even before we became human beings,
   standing upright on the planet,
even before the universe itself
   arose out of nothingness,
in your infinite love
you were thinking and dreaming of each one of us?

Is it true that since the beginning of time,
even before your son,
   your Word,
   came among us,
even before he was announced
   by the prophets,
you saw us in him,
   and you loved all of us already
   as your sons and daughters?

Is it true that at the dawn of time
   you gave us this earth,
   not to a few people but to all,

167

a single homeland with many faces,
so that we might live on it together
    and transform it together?

Is it true that when Jesus appeared,
    a man like us,
    as our brother he welcomed all of us,
    unconditionally,
    carrying us in his heart,
    so far,
    so deep,
that we were incorporated in him,
becoming members of his body,
    so that in future
    we could no longer touch anyone among us
    without hearing him say: 'It is I'?

And finally,
    is it true
    that all of us, in him,
    having passed through death
have entered with him into the resurrection
and are invited to live forever with our Father,
    as a united family,
    loving him and loving ourselves,
    in the love of our heavenly home?

If it's true, Lord,
    and I believe that it is true,
how can we call any man or woman
a stranger,
since all of us are sons and daughters of the same Father,
    and all are brothers and sisters to one another?

. . . And by what right do we dare,
    oh God forgive us,
to decide that this or that territory
    is ours forever,
    and people must have visas to enter it;
that we have a right to this job,

and that nobody can take it away from us
unless we refuse to take it on
because we think it's beneath us;
that this person deserves to be welcomed,
while the other person
should be deported ?
My God, how can we
mutilate the body of your son,
and while mutilating his body
inflict mortal injuries on ourselves,
how can we do this without tearing your family apart?

Forgive us, Lord, and understand us!
The earth you gave us
was so big for us when we were small,
that we have grown up
at a distance from each other.

We are of different colours,
we have different languages,
different customs.
We have made false gods for ourselves,
often unaware that we have only one God
and that this God is our Father.
Today, at last,
it is possible for all of us to know one another
and even to visit one another;
but what happens when someone—one of us—
turns up and we have never met before?
We are indifferent or hostile,
we refer to that person as a stranger . . .
instead of being overjoyed
and happy that we can embrace an unknown brother or
sister.
Nevertheless, Father,
you have always dreamed
that such meetings would be cause for celebration,
and your son has told us
that we will be judged on how we receive people,

whether or not we know
that he is there in the unknown brother or sister.[1]

I know Lord, and I'm ashamed
because I don't live my life on the basis of what I know.
Because while I proclaim loudly,
and sometimes very loudly indeed,
during certain discussions:
I'm not a racist!
at the same time I often think, very quietly,
that there are limits, however . . .
that it is our duty to preserve . . . !
that in the circumstances . . .
and I discover that the solid walls in my heart
are still standing.

Help me, Lord,
help me to change my self-centred heart
into a heart that reaches out to others,
so that nobody will ever be excluded
from my communion.
Help me to respect people who are different,
without wanting to mould them in my own image,
for I remain arrogantly convinced
that my image
is the appropriate one for all men and women.
In front of my brothers and sisters who look so unlike me,
help me to acknowledge
how small and poor I am
unless I am enriched
by their diversity.
Help me to grasp all the opportunities of meeting them,
opportunities that are so numerous today;
help me to come out of myself
and to go towards others,
making neighbours of those far away from me.

Help me not to judge and still less to condemn
those who have suffered

1. Mat. 25:31–46

more seriously than I
because of brothers and sisters who are different.
Help me to see the difficulties clearly,
   and without denying the problems,
   to fight where I am,
   in whatever way I can,
   so that there may never be rules
   or laws
that prevent us, unknown brothers and sisters,
   from meeting each other.

And help me to be more open every day to the *life* of
                                        your son,
   because I believe
   that it is this offered *life*
   which makes us brothers and sisters.
Then, Lord,
as a faithful artisan on your project of love,
   I will be able to repeat each evening,
   as I say good night to you:
   'our FATHER'.

Whoever loves his brother lives in the light, and so there is nothing in him that will cause someone else to sin. But whoever hates his brother is in the darkness; he walks in it and does not know where he is going, because the darkness has made him blind (1 Jn. 2:10–11).

It is through faith that all of you are God's sons in union with Christ Jesus. You were baptized into union with Christ, and now you are clothed, so to speak, with the life of Christ himself. So there is no difference between Jews and Gentiles, between slaves and free men, between men and women, you are all one in union with Christ Jesus (Gal. 3:26–28).

34. Lord, I'm incapable of giving my whole life, bit by bit

If something is useless, we throw it out. Now, we want our lives to be useful to our loved ones, but we also want them to be useful to all our brothers and sisters. There is so much to be done on this earth where so many men and women are crushed by suffering in so many forms!

Who hasn't dreamt at one time or another of 'giving' his or her whole life to others and to the Lord? But we come up against our own limitations and we resign ourselves to them very quickly, thinking that total generosity is reserved to heroes and saints.

We are frightened by the long haul. Is it possible to give every day, every moment of our lives? Humanly speaking the answer is no, but with Christ it is yes, because we can give him everything: the best of ourselves, the less good aspects also, and even the sin. And from the fullness but also from the emptiness of our lives, he can make an offering.

I believe, Lord,
that I'd be capable of accomplishing
some extraordinary feats
   . . . once in a while:
something that would mobilize all my resources,
   because I'd be upset by destitution,
   because I'd be shocked by injustice,
   because one of my loved ones would be in danger.
I even believe sometimes
that I'd be capable of risking my life,
   or even of giving my life,
   in one go, at one stroke,
for my ideal,
for my love,
   for my child,
   and perhaps even for someone else's child.
And while this thought, alas,
   tempts me secretly
to admire myself just a little,
   it also reassures me,

because you have told us, Lord,
   that to give one's life to others
is the greatest possible proof of love.

But the thing that humiliates me
is that I'm incapable of giving my life
   bit by bit,
   a morsel at a time,
   day after day,
   hour by hour,
   minute by minute,
   giving,
   always giving,
   . . . and giving myself.
I'm not able to do that,
although I know perfectly well that it's what you ask of me.

What you want of me is so simple, Lord!
   It's too simple
   . . . and too difficult.
You want me to do what I have to do, every day,
   to take a small step, then another,
   and still another one tomorrow,
   in the course of my everyday routine;
to go through every day together with those who are close
                                             to me,
   my husband, my wife, my children,
   my colleagues at work,
   my neighbours,
   and all the people I meet;
to struggle, every moment of every day,
   to live
   as you want me to live,
and together with others, to fight
so that all human beings may live as human beings.
A thousand little bits of life to be given each day
   in the thousand ways that love can be expressed,
   but which are so usual
   that they are no longer seen,
   so ordinary

that they are no longer noticed.
But you have told me that you need them
     to make them into an offering,
and so that one day I'll be able to say truthfully:
I've given my whole life for my brothers and sisters.

That's what you want, Lord,
     . . . but it's beyond me.

Why did you invent endurance, Lord,
     and faithfulness in small things,
     and love that is always demanding?
I've dreamed of giving my whole life to another person,
     one other,
     and to others,
and I thought
that one *yes* would be sufficient,
     just one gesture,
     one offering,
but I've discovered that it would take thousands
and maybe millions.
I've dreamed of a life that would blaze up
in some great deeds,
     and then found out
     that the fire must burn
     slowly,
fed by tiny twigs
which keep the flame alight
so that it is never extinguished.

Always beginning again,
     always.

Lord, I can't,
     and I know
     and I'm afraid
     that when I look at my life,
     in your presence, in the light of your Spirit,
I'll discover that for the few moments I've given
there will be thousands that I've refused to give

174

. . . and I won't have given my whole life . . .
   but only
   a few little bits of it.

It's true, my child, says the Lord,
   that circumstances
allow some people
to give all their light
   in a few scintillating flashes,
   but many are asked
to kindle a thousand small lights of love
   in the deep night of their times.
   Don't have regrets about this.
   Don't judge.
For who is to say that millions of candles
lit during a long life
don't produce more light
than a fireworks display?

In addition, my child,
I don't ask you to succeed always,
   only to try always.
And above all
I ask you to accept your own limitations,
to acknowledge your poverty and give it to me,
because when you give your life
you give not only your wealth
   but also your poverty,
   and even your sins.
Do this, my child,
and with the little bits of life you have wasted
and withheld from all those who were waiting,
   I will complete what is lacking in you
   and restore your capacity for endurance,
   because in my hands
   the poverty you offer will become wealth,
   . . . for eternity.

*Then Jesus called the crowd and his disciples to him. 'If anyone
wants to come with me,' he told them, 'he must forget self, carry*

his cross, and follow me. For whoever wants to save his own life will lose it; but whoever loses his life for me and for the gospel will save it. Does a person gain anything if he wins the whole world but loses his life? Of course not! There is nothing he can give to regain his life' (Mk. 8:34–37).

But God's mercy is so abundant, and his love for us is so great, that while we were spiritually dead in our disobedience he brought us to life with Christ. It is by God's grace that you have been saved. In our union with Christ Jesus he raised us up with him to rule with him in the heavenly world (Eph. 2:4–6).

35. We haven't finished loving each other

For husbands and wives who have loved each other and lived their lives together, nothing is harder than the separation of death. However, they haven't finished loving each other, because the loved one who is gone is still living in another life beyond death, and love cannot die when it is an authentic love in Christ.

But loving without the physical presence of the loved one is a terrible trial, a 'purgatory'—the last purification of love before people meet again in eternity. Happy are those who though left alone continue to be faithful and continue to live out their love (which does not mean, of course, that to rebuild one's life is to be unfaithful). To their children and to all those who have doubts about love or don't even know what love is, such people may testify that love can live and flourish beyond the two bodies of those who go through life together. They can also testify that at the final stage of its development such love is totally gratuitous: 'I miss him, but I'm glad he's happy!'

May such love help those who lack love!

I woke up, Lord
   . . . and he wasn't there any longer.
I turned over in bed
   . . . but his place was empty,
and my lonely fingers were still searching for his.

My love is with you;
   I believe he is, this is what I hope for,
but, Lord, I can't
   get used to his absence.
I'm torn apart every time I wake up,
   just as waking up
shatters the patient whose legs have been amputated.

   He's not there any longer!

I won't hear him any more,
I'll no longer share

the day's work with him.
I'll never again go over the furrows and wrinkles
   on his beloved face,
   furrows and wrinkles where I used to glean life,
   the last grains of life
   which day after day,
   in joy and in sorrow,
   we planted
   and harvested,
   a thousand fruits of love.
I'll never again search in the depths of his eyes
for the soft light of his twilight gaze,
   after the bright morning,
   the blazing midday fires,
   and the occasional shadows
   of days when clouds built up
   and the storm erupted,
before the rainbow of peace
rose in our hearts.

We loved each other . . . but Lord,
we haven't finished loving each other!
We loved each other, Lord,
but we lived together;
he was in me and I was in him,
and you,
   you sealed our two lives together
   so that they became one.
But he has gone to those distant shores
   that no one can reach
   without passing through death,
and from the shore where I'm standing, with my feet on
this earth,
I can't even catch a glimpse of him.
   Oh my beloved . . . gone,
   far away,
   in the mists of infinity.

   He's not there any longer!

They say that one gets used to it, Lord,
that time does its work,
    but I know now
that neither time nor death can vanquish love,
    because one morning I whispered *always*,
    and he said to me *always*,
    and you promised us
that we would love each other forever.
Without seeing, Lord,
I want to believe,
    I do believe.

We haven't finished loving each other!

Yesterday we were together,
    every day,
    learning about living,
because while each of us was seeking the other's happiness,
    often we were seeking our own;
sometimes we gave and sometimes we took from the other,
    but through our constant efforts
    our love was increased.

Today we have entered into purgatory.
    I suffer because I'm alone,
    he suffers because he's far away;
    how could he be happy without me
    when I'm so unhappy without him!
But he is purifying our love
in your light, Lord,
    whereas for me
    it is during the night
    that I must perfect it.

Help me, my God,
to love him even more today
    in his absence
    than yesterday in his presence;
to love him for himself, expecting nothing in return,
    happy that he's happy,

close beside you;
and gaining nothing for myself
except joy in his joy.

Yes, my love is intact in my living heart.
    Death can do nothing to it,
    and that's why I'm suffering;
    because my spring has not run dry,
    it flows and overflows,
and I have loving words to spare,
    and a thousand gestures of affection,
smiles stored up that remain unemployed,
and tears falling like rain, which flood my heart
    and make all these flowers of love
    spring up more quickly still.

Lord, I won't allow them
    to wither,
    to fade,
    in my closed heart.
I'll gather them every day,
a wonderful harvest for my children
    and my grandchildren,
    my friends,
    my neighbours,
    and all the forgotten beggars
    who search for fragments of love
    on the wayside.

But my suffering, Lord,
is still my suffering!
The dreadful loneliness and the long days
and the deep night,
    the *absence*,
the cruel absence,
the deep void into which my distraught heart plunges
without reaching the bottom.
    I miss him. Lord, do you understand ?
    I miss him!
    Why have you abandoned me?

Forgive me, Lord,
forgive me for being despondent,
you who beckon to me from your cross every day.
It's when I forget to look at you
    that the night overwhelms me.
    You are waiting for me
    and he is there beside you, watching me,
    and with his love he invites me,
    guides me and supports me.

Thanks to you, Lord,
thanks to him,
my suffering won't be lost,
because I'll offer the superabundance of love
    that my suffering demands of me,
    love which lives and grows, beyond my suffering;
I'll offer it for those young explorers of love
    who seek without finding,
    losing their way,
    innocents,
    caught in the mirage of the moment;
for those who don't know, Lord,
that loving means
    leaving selfishness aside so as to give one's self to the
                                                            other,
    and being ready to receive the other's gift of himself;
for those who don't know
that love is often suffering
    before it is joy,
joy in the new life which takes flesh
    when two lives join together,
    without ever destroying the love they share;
for those who don't know
that love is forever,
    and that only you can give
    this love its infinite dimension.

I'd like to say this to them, Lord,
    to say it to them through my life,
and since my beloved is waiting for me, beside you,

in peace, I also
will await our meeting,
and of this engagement,
of this cruel and sweet engagement,
of this waiting I'll make an offering
before I'm taken into the arms of my faithful love,
    before we love each other at last,
    Lord,
    in your house,
    infinitely, eternally.

. . . *and if Christ has not been raised from death, then we have
nothing to preach and you have nothing to believe. . .For if the
dead are not raised, neither has Christ been raised. And if Christ
has not been raised, then your faith is a delusion and you are still
lost in your sins. It would also mean that the believers in Christ
who have died are lost. If our hope in Christ is good for this life
only and no more, then we deserve more pity than anyone else in
all the world* (1 Cor. 15:14, 16–19).

'Do not be worried and upset,' Jesus told them. 'Believe in God
and believe also in me. There are many rooms in my Father's
house, and I am going to prepare a place for you. I would not tell
you this if it were not so' (Jn. 14.1–3).

36. I'll let you take me in your arms, Lord!

Many 'expressions of faith', accepted and repeated without any explanation, are very clumsy and sometimes they are false: especially those related to suffering. The people who use them are sincere, of course, and it is to be hoped that they discover the real meaning despite the inexactitude of the words. But for non-believers who go no further than the words, they are shocking. Many have distanced themselves from the 'good' God presented to them in this way, a God who appears to them to be a monster. Suffering is always a bad thing, a 'waste'. God does not rejoice in suffering, he bears it. But he hasn't left us alone to deal with suffering. Jesus Christ has 'salvaged the waste'. Bearing his own sufferings, he has borne ours with them. He made them the raw material of redemption. But be careful, Jesus Christ didn't save the world through his suffering, but through the love with which he bore his suffering and ours. Love is the only thing that saves, and love is the only thing which gives life.

When we are faced with suffering we must fight with all our strength to overcome it. When it refuses to surrender in our lives, we must ask the Lord to allow us to share it with him. He has already suffered our suffering. So let us allow him to carry us and to carry our pain at the same time. And then during the night may we offer, not our suffering—one doesn't offer 'waste'—but our faith in his saving love.

I was watching them, Lord . . .

They were two little friends,
but they were fighting with each other today.
They fell,
both of them slightly hurt,
   they cried,
   sobbed,
   and . . .
the two mothers came running.
One of them tried to take her child in her arms,
but he pushed her away furiously, hitting her.
   He was by himself,

closed in,
locked in,
and still crying.
The other child let himself be swept up
in a swirl of affection.
　　His mother covered him with kisses.
　　His tears dried up.
From time to time he smiled, saying:
　　'It's sore, it hurts!'
His injuries were in fact more severe than those of the
　　　　　　　　　　　　　　　　　　　other child.

　　Lord,
there are people who say
that the more one suffers the more one is loved by God.
　　That's not true, is it?
You can't love more or less,
since you love all of us personally
　　and all of us infinitely,
　　but when we suffer,
　　your love,
　　like that of a loving mother,
　　becomes something closer to us,
　　more available to us.
And like little children
　　we can let you carry us
　　and our sufferings,
　　or we can push you away
　　and stay alone, overwhelmed, in a state of shock.

It is thus that great suffering
can bring us closer to God
or take us farther away from him.

Many have gone away, Lord . . .
They didn't believe in your love.
And there are also those who watch helplessly
while their loved ones suffer cruelly,
more of them, perhaps,
than of those who suffer themselves.

And I,
arrogantly,
full of self confidence,
I say that I believe!

But it's easy for me to say it,
I'm not suffering.
    And I know
that if the day comes when I am crucified
by terrible pain,
    I'll implore,
    I'll cry out,
    and perhaps,
    like the hurt child,
    I will rebel also!

So, am I accusing you, Lord ? . . .
as if you wanted suffering
and sent it to us,
    you who desire our happiness,
    you who give us life.

Perhaps I'll ask myself
what I did to deserve such suffering.
As if you punished us,
    like ineffective school teachers
    who punish their pupils,
    like parents unable to make themselves heard or
                                        respected
    who compensate by severity
    for their own imperfections.
As if we didn't punish ourselves enough
    and you had to add something more,
    like parents smacking disobedient children
    who get hurt when they fall . . .
    and who suffer.

Perhaps I'll demand a miracle?
as if you didn't give all human beings
the freedom

to build their lives,
to fight against the evils of the world,
to struggle against sin,
which mysteriously,
implacably,
corrupts the world
and gives rise to innumerable sufferings.

Perhaps I would be treating you as if you were insensitive,
you the good God?
As if you didn't suffer
   when you see us suffering,
just as those who love suffer
   when they see their loved ones suffering!

Since I can turn to you today, Lord
with hands and heart
free from the constraints of pain,
   I pray you,
   I implore you,
beyond the pious and false considerations
   that cause some of the faithful to go on their knees,
   but cause so many others
   to tremble with indignation,
   I ask you for an explanation!

Then on the day of great tribulation,
perhaps I'll understand
that in itself
suffering is never a grace,
   never
because it is a 'waste'
   to be salvaged from a world
   and from an imperfect humanity,
   because they are only creatures
   and because they need to be redeemed by you,
   to be re-created by you.

Perhaps I'll understand
   that you,

Jesus,
  didn't bless your own suffering
  or welcome it as a gift,
that you didn't seek it out,
  but that you endured it.

Because it fell on you,
my Jesus,
your cross fell on you!
  The cross on your shoulders,
  YOU on the cross,
  fastened to it,
  nailed to it,
  with no possibility of escape.
  YOU, body and soul crucified,
  defenceless,
  trembling with fear and pain,
  you cried out,
  imploring your Father to perform a miracle . . .
  and he didn't do it . . .
  he couldn't do it,
for how could a father prevent his son
from being in solidarity with his brothers and sisters,
to the very end!

So, let me believe
with all my strength
that you didn't come among us to take away our sufferings,
  but to live them with us,
after helping us to fight against them.
Because at that time, Jesus,
  you were carrying
  not only your cross
  but our crosses also,
  the big ones and the small ones,
  those of yesterday,
  of today,
  of tomorrow,
  those of all humankind,
  because you love us,

and as victim of your love
all human suffering
became your suffering.

Oh great and loving Jesus,
your love was needed to carry all those crosses,
    to the very end.
Your infinite love was needed
    to lift them,
    to raise them up,
body raised above earth
spirit raised up to heaven.
The omnipotence of your love was needed
    to penetrate them,
    to burn them,
    to disintegrate them
    and to liberate *life*.
Because it's not the dead wood
which gives heat and light,
    it's the flame.
It's not the dead wood that should be offered,
but *the fire*,
the *fire of love* which burns *everything*.

But I'm not suffering today, Lord!. . .
    And if tomorrow
    I can do nothing else . . .
        except to suffer,
I ask you in advance
to give me the courage
to offer my powerlessness,
and then, like the hurt child,
I'll let you take me in your arms,
    and your love will carry me
    to eternity!

If a person is tempted by such trials, he must not say, 'This temp-
tation comes from God.' For God cannot be tempted by evil, and
he himself tempts no one. But a person is tempted when he is
drawn away and trapped by his own evil desire. Then his evil

188

desire conceives and gives birth to sin; and sin, when it is full-grown, gives birth to death (Jas. 1:13–15).

But he endured the suffering that should have been ours,
the pain that we should have borne.
All the while we thought that his suffering
was punishment sent by God.
But because of our sins he was wounded,
beaten because of the evil we did . . . (Is. 53:4–5).

But God's mercy is so abundant, and his love for us is so great, that while we were spiritually dead in our disobedience he brought us to life with Christ. It is by God's grace that you have been saved. In our union with Christ Jesus he raised us up with him to rule with him in the heavenly world (Eph. 2:4–6).